Shifting Sands

A Guidebook for Crossing the Deserts of Change

Steve Donahue

BERRETT-KOEHLER PUBLISHERS, INC.
San Francisco

Berrett-Koehler Publishers, Inc.
235 Montgomery Street, Suite 650
San Francisco, CA 94104-2916
Tel: (415) 288-0260   Fax: (415) 362-2512   www.bkconnection.com

Ordering Information

Quantity sales. Special discounts are available on quantity purchases by corporations, associations, and others. For details, contact the "Special Sales Department" at the Berrett-Koehler address above.

Individual sales. Berrett-Koehler publications are available through most bookstores. They can also be ordered directly from Berrett-Koehler: Tel: (800) 929-2929; Fax: (802) 864-7626; www.bkconnection.com

Orders for college textbook/course adoption use. Please contact Berrett-Koehler: Tel: (800) 929-2929; Fax: (802) 864-7626.

Orders by U.S. trade bookstores and wholesalers. Please contact Publishers Group West, 1700 Fourth Street, Berkeley, CA 94710. Tel: (510) 528-1444; Fax (510) 528-3444.

Berrett-Koehler and the BK logo are registered trademarks of Berrett-Koehler Publishers, Inc.

Printed in the United States of America

Berrett-Koehler books are printed on long-lasting acid-free paper. When it is available, we choose paper that has been manufactured by environmentally responsible processes. These may include using trees grown in sustainable forests, incorporating recycled paper, minimizing chlorine in bleaching, or recycling the energy produced at the paper mill.

Library of Congress Cataloging-in-Publication Data are available.

First Edition
09 08 07 06 05 04   10 9 8 7 6 5 4 3 2 1

Illustration credits:
Map: Hugh D'Andrade (www.hughillustration.com); Photographs not otherwise credited were taken by the author.

Developmental Editing: Ocean Lum. Copyediting: Elissa Rabellino. Design and production: Richard Wilson. Indexing: Rachel Rice. Proofreading: Carolyn Uno.

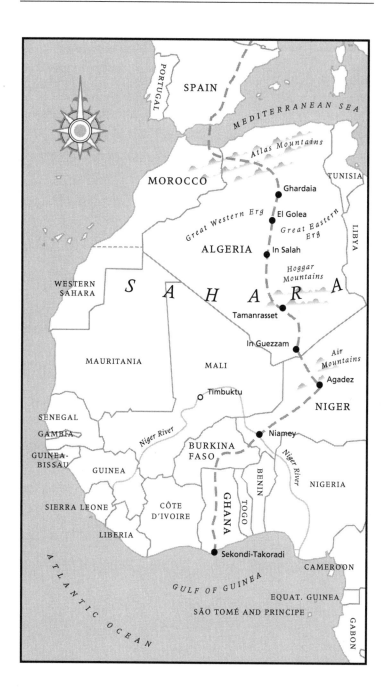

The first speech I gave about the Sahara Desert caught me by surprise. I was hired to address the meeting of an association of asphalt-road builders who were notorious for being a difficult audience. I had no idea what to talk about. Then I remembered the paved road that crosses part of the Sahara. At a certain point the road ends. You aren't really anywhere—it just stops. Life is like that, too. Sometimes the paved road you've been speeding along quite comfortably suddenly ends and you're in a desert. I was surprised by how much the road builders liked the story and the slides. I decided to focus on presentations about crossing the Sahara, and my speaking career took off.

My next surprise about the power of the desert metaphor came from an unlikely source: a mountain climber. He was a motivational speaker who sat next to me on an airplane, and his claim to fame was climbing Mount Everest. On more than one occasion a prospective client had hired him instead of me. He charged twice as much as I did and was three times as busy. I had a bad case of professional jealousy. But he seemed friendly enough, and after a couple of drinks I began to relax. Then he told me that he planned to cross the Arabian Desert, write a book about the adventure, and start giving speeches about crossing deserts. I ordered another drink.

Alcohol combined with the lack of oxygen in an airplane triggers air rage in some passengers. Others react to the mix of booze and altitude with a more common side effect: air blabber. Suddenly your mouth has a mind of its own. The person next to you becomes a combination of therapist, long-lost friend, and spiritual advisor. Fortunately we were both afflicted with air blabber. We began conversing in earnest. He asked me practical questions about crossing deserts. I asked him a question he'd probably heard a thousand times.

"How big is the top of Mount Everest?"

"About the size of a small kitchen table," he responded.

"That's amazing," I said. "You know, when you cross the Sahara Desert, there is no way of knowing where the desert ends. There's no peak, no border, no sign that says, 'You Are Now Leaving the Sahara Desert—Have a Nice Day!'"

He laughed and shook his head. "I guess I'll find out soon enough that mountains and deserts are much different from one another."

When the plane landed, it was very late. We mumbled some farewells and promised to stay in touch. Waiting for my luggage to appear, I couldn't stop thinking of mountains and deserts. They are two of the most powerful symbols we have. Throughout history, most cultures and most of the world's major religions have used these symbols to illustrate values and teachings. My speaking colleague was right—they are literally not the same. And they are also metaphorically quite different.

Was it possible that we struggle in times of change because the ever-shifting quality of life defies the goal-setting, strategic-planning approach of the mountain-climbing metaphor? The divorce I was struggling with at that time was certainly not going according to plan. Many of the people I spoke to in large corporations undergoing mergers and reorganizations seemed to suffer all the more from setting goals that couldn't be reached or making plans that kept changing. I wondered if life and its inevitable transitions could be less upsetting and even more fulfilling if we stopped thinking about everything as a goal to achieve that simply required the right map to get us to the summit.

Several years and a few metaphorical deserts later, I am just as surprised to have written a book about my wonderings and my wanderings. I hope my ideas and experiences help you cross your own deserts of change.

Acknowledgments

There are many people who assisted or inspired me in writing this book. I'd like to thank the following:

George Donahue, my dad, for bringing me a T-shirt from virtually every country he visited on business, and for making travel seem exotic and exciting.

Julie Donahue, my mom, for encouraging me to follow my heart, even if it meant that I'd probably spend most of my life living far away from her.

Chloé and Spirit, my kids, for making me laugh when I needed to.

Pamela Mountjoy, my friend, for believing in this book more than I did at times and for being the glue that held me and this book together from start to finish.

Carol Roth, my literary agent, for her steadfast belief in the power of my story and her determination to find the right publisher.

Tom Bowes and the staff at InCourage, for seeing new ways to share the desert metaphor with organizations in transition.

Ocean Lum, my first-draft editor, for her discerning intellect, which kept me focused on a coherent message.

Linda Davidson and her team at Canspeak, for encouraging me to pick up my pen and finally start writing.

Bobby Neufeld, my friend and mountaineering companion, for taking me into the high country and defending the spirit of real mountain climbers when I got carried away with my metaphor.

Judith Moser, my friend, for her support and insights as I've crossed my own deserts of change.

Tallis, Henri, and André, my desert traveling companions, for accompanying me on this journey that profoundly influenced my life. My apologies to Henri for changing his name to Jean-Luc; I found that my English-speaking audiences were confusing the French pronunciation of Henri with André. I hope that no offense will be taken, for none was intended.

Steve Donahue
Victoria, British Columbia
January 2004

Are You Crossing a Desert or Climbing a Mountain?

Upon the endless sand dunes
The camel shall always rule.
But it's wiser in the mountains
To ride a stubborn mule.
—Desert proverb

The Sahara is the largest desert on earth, covering an area approximately the size of the United States. My buddy Tallis and I were halfway across it, camped on a rocky hill in open desert a thousand miles south of the Mediterranean, with another thousand miles of sand dunes and sandstorms ahead of us. We were quite literally in the middle of nowhere.

The blistering Saharan sun had just set, bringing the evening's cool relief. But we both knew that within an hour the temperature would drop almost 40 degrees, and by midnight we'd be shivering in our sleeping bags beneath a breathtaking canopy of icy stars. We were several miles south of the

Algerian oasis of Tamanrasset. We had no vehicle. We didn't know how we were going to continue heading south across this seemingly endless desert. I didn't know when or if we'd make it to the other side. I didn't even know where the other side was. It wasn't in Algeria—I knew that much. Was it in Niger?

"Where does the Sahara actually end?" I wondered aloud.

"Are you talking to me?" Tallis asked.

"Not really; just wondering if we'll ever make it across this desert, and if we do, how long it will take."

"I haven't a clue. We may never make it to the other side. All I care about right now is getting this fire started so we can cook some dinner before it's completely dark."

Tallis busied himself with the fire. The predictably cloudless sky was bluish black above us, and a single bright star already sparkled. To the west, the sky was still glowing, like a blast furnace whose fuel supply was being quickly shut off.

Tallis looked up from the fire and scanned the horizon.

"Shit!"

"What?"

I followed his finger to a speck on a distant dune. As soon as I saw it, I scrambled to my feet and quickly started dousing the fire with sand.

Life, especially during a time of change, is like crossing the Sahara. The journey seems endless; we get lost, we get stuck, and we chase mirages. While crossing the Sahara, it's difficult to tell when you've arrived at the other side. Much of life is like that. You can't see your goal. You can't tell when you've arrived. What is the goal of life itself?

Being a parent is like crossing the Sahara. How do you

know when you're done raising your children? When they move out? When they get married? When they stop borrowing money? When they forgive you for being imperfect? Even those who have lost a child remain parents because they will always carry the pain that is unique to one who loses a child. Parenting is endless. And while it is for many of us the most rewarding experience of our lives, there is no mountaintop, no summit we can look down from and say, "I've made it. My job of parenting is over."

The never-ending, never-arriving aspect of life can frustrate us because our dominant cultural metaphor is more about climbing mountains. We live in a goal-oriented, achievement-focused, results-driven culture. Defining problems, setting targets, and implementing plans are seen as the solutions to any and all of our challenges. This is a mountain-climbing ethos.

Mountain climbers can see their goal. The peak is visible. It inspires and guides them to the top. If you reach the summit, there's little doubt about your achievement—you know when you've made it. Mountain climbing is about the destination. It means that you have a goal that is tangible, with a describable end result. Saving for retirement is a good example of climbing a mountain. Your goal is definable. You know how much money you will need to retire in comfort.

However, if your goal is vague, is difficult to describe, or sounds more like a way of being than an end result, you are crossing a desert. Think of marriage. Couples never say, "Let's get married and see if we can reach the 50-year mark." People marry to be happy, to support one another, to have a family, and to share life together. These reasons describe a way of being, not some specific end result. Deserts are about the journey. So marriage is a desert.

Mountain climbers not only have a clear goal, but they have an idea of how long it will take to reach the summit. They plan on a specific time frame for accomplishing their objective. A financial planner can show you how long it will take to reach your retirement goals based on your finances and lifestyle.

But there's no such thing as a divorce planner, who can print out a timetable outlining when you'll finally be healed from the pain of that desert. No one knows when a midlife crisis will be finished. Members of Alcoholics Anonymous still call themselves alcoholics even if they haven't touched a drop in 30 years. Deserts seem endless, or at least it's very difficult to predict how long it will take to cross them.

Mountain-climbing techniques don't work in the desert. To successfully cross the Sahara or a desert of life, you need to follow the rules of desert travel. But first you need to know the difference between a mountain and a desert.

I n the waning twilight, the glowing western sky outlined a distant figure moving steadily toward us, along the ridge of a sand dune. His erect posture, graceful movement, and long blue robes told me he was a Tuareg, one of the famed nomads of the central and southern Sahara. They are also known as the "blue men of the desert," for the cobalt hue of their dark skin, which comes from the dye in the turbans, or *cheches*, that cover their faces and heads.

"Leave the fire alone," Tallis cautioned. "He'll think we're afraid."

"I am afraid!" I shot back.

"He's already seen it, anyway. Just relax. It looks like he's alone."

The Tuareg first appeared in the Sahara a thousand years ago. No one knows where they came from. The fact that their origins have remained a mystery only adds to the romantic image of the noble desert nomad. A warrior people, they ruled this harsh land for more than a millennium, often clashing among themselves before the French arrived in the 1860s. The Tuareg considered the French cowards for using rifles, and they attacked the French with drawn sabers, riding their fleetest camels. They were eventually subdued in the early 1900s, but many of the Tuareg continue their nomadic lifestyle, often ignoring the borders that define postcolonial Sahara.

The nomad arrived at our campsite a few minutes later. He was slim, with a fine aquiline nose and a regal bearing. He spoke to us in heavily accented French.

"Un peu de sel, s'il vous plaît."

I anxiously searched around in our kitchen supplies and gave him all our remaining salt. I knew that salt was precious in this part of the desert. It was literally worth its weight in gold during certain periods of the caravan trade. Without a word he was gone, and we watched as he retraced his steps into the desert evening.

"Do you think he's alone?" I nervously asked Tallis.

"How should I know? I'm no expert on Tuaregs."

"I heard that they carry a really nasty dagger underneath those blue robes," I said.

"Well, we're in trouble if he uses that dagger. We've got nothing to defend ourselves with but this frying pan," Tallis responded.

"What if he comes back? What if he's not alone? What if he doesn't want salt at all and he's just checking us out?"

"Would you stop with the questions!" Tallis snapped. "I don't know. No one knows. We are in the middle of the Sahara Desert. There is at least one nomad in the area—maybe more. That's all we know."

"Yeah, but I can't stand not knowing what he wants or what to do if he comes back. I can't stand not knowing how we're going to get out of this place. We don't have a car. We don't have a plan. We don't know what we're doing tomorrow or the next day. We just sit and wait for something to happen."

"Like I said, we're in the middle of the Sahara Desert," Tallis shot back emphatically.

"Shhh! What's that?"

"Someone's coming!"

Preparedness, planning, and past experience make a difference when it comes to climbing a mountain or completing a project. If you're building a new house, you hire a contractor with a proven record. The builder constructs your home from a plan by a reputable designer or architect. Delays and challenges may arise, but there is an obvious link between the three Ps and your chances of success when you start climbing toward a goal.

Deserts are different. The Sahara can frustrate a Land Rover full of German engineers with a GPS guidance system and enough spare parts to build a new vehicle from

A Tuareg nomad.

scratch. On the other hand, a beat-up VW camper with bald tires can take half a dozen ill-prepared students safely over unmapped dunes and past bandits to the sun-drenched beaches of West Africa.

Experience and preparedness don't guarantee success or swiftness in the deserts of life. A skilled therapist can be stopped in her tracks by her own midlife crisis. Her knowledge, degrees, and experience can't help. The counselor needs counseling because she is in a desert.

In a desert it's normal to feel inept. Your problem isn't lack of planning. If planning really helped and if training really mattered, we'd take lessons on marriage as well as divorce. You'd need a license to have children. There'd be a test to pass, and you'd need to submit a plan for your child's growth and learning before receiving permission to procreate.

Unpredictability and uncertainty are two hallmarks of desert travel. What is the route to raising a teenager? How can you predict what the economy will do to your struggling business? Like relentless sandstorms that torment you no matter how much you cover yourself, uncertainty is impossible to avoid in the deserts of life.

Anytime our lives seem uncertain and unpredictable, and planning and experience have limited value, we are in a desert. This is perhaps the most stressful and agonizing aspect of deserts and the main reason why we prefer mountains; mountains are less ambiguous. Running your first marathon is a difficult mountain to climb. There's no guarantee that you'll finish. But how to train for and run a marathon is mapped out and documented. The challenge is with your body and willpower rather than the shadowy foe of uncertainty. Better the enemy I can see than the one who is sneaking up on me.

F ootsteps scrambling up the loose rock on the path to our campsite were getting closer.

"We need a plan. I think we can handle two or maybe even three of them," I whispered to Tallis.

"Don't be ridiculous!" he scolded. "There's nothing we can do."

I continued as if I hadn't heard him. "They'll be here any second. I'll throw sand on the fire and you grab the frying pan and start swinging."

"What if I hit you instead of them? Relax—let's just see what they want."

I turned around and the Tuareg who had come before was standing there. He was alone, holding out his hand.

"Un peu de poivre, s'il vous plaît."

It had grown dark, so I used my flashlight to locate the pepper shaker. I passed it to him, hoping that he wouldn't see my hand trembling. I noticed his eyes quickly survey the rest of our supplies. Without a word he turned away from the faint light of our small fire. The night quickly swallowed him up.

Neither of us knew what to make of it. The nomad's actions seemed innocent enough; it wasn't much different from your neighbor borrowing a cup of sugar. But I'd read how the Tuareg would approach caravans, posing as friendly guides. Often numbering in the thousands of camels, the cara- vans would be strung out for miles across the desert. After identifying the most vulnerable sections of the train, the Tuareg would take their leave, returning later to attack and rob the caravan of everything of value.

"So much for your frying pan plan," Tallis grumbled.

"Did you see him? He's checking us out. It's the Tuareg version of casing the joint. We've got to take some action. Either we get out of here while we have a chance, or we prepare to defend ourselves. Maybe we should sneak up on them and see what they're doing."

"Just cool it! We don't even know if there's more than one of them! We have to sit tight. We'll cook some dinner and sleep in shifts."

At that moment I hated the Sahara Desert. I hated Peter O'Toole for making deserts and nomads seem so romantic in *Lawrence of Arabia.* This wasn't romantic at all. I hated feeling so alone, so exposed and ill prepared, in a place of such uncertainty. Straining to hear any new sounds of footsteps, I began opening a can of beans. Tallis put the remainder of our twigs on the fire.

Most of us don't like vagueness, ambiguity, or paradox. We don't like being lost or asking for directions. Uncertainty isn't tolerated well in our society. Western culture, and in particular North American culture, is about knowing where you are and getting the job done.

To be fair, our problem-solving, goal-setting, and persevering attitude has helped us accomplish great things. The can-do credo of Western society has cured horrible diseases, put a man on the moon, built the Panama Canal, and invented heated toilet seats. Our culture has perfected the art of achievement. We know how to "just do it."

But much of life is not at all about achievement, success, or goals. Life is often about being lost, finding ourselves, getting stuck, getting unstuck, following a mirage, and then finding our way for a while until we get lost again. Much of life is like a desert, not a mountain.

There are two kinds of metaphorical deserts. The first and most noticeable is a desert of change. This is a period of significant, fundamental, and sometimes rapid change. Deserts of change include such transitions as divorce, losing your job, the death of a loved one, a career change, starting a new business, becoming a stay-at-home parent, reentering the workforce after being a stay-at-home parent, a merger or reorganization at work, coming out of the closet, caring for an ailing parent, or a midlife crisis, to name just a few. Deserts of change may seem endless while you are in the midst of them, but in hindsight they are finite and usually more intense than the other type—the desert of life.

A desert of life is also a time of transition, but the change is more gradual and less noticeable because it is spread out over a longer period. Raising a family, marriage, a career, and retirement are some examples. Deserts of change can seem like interruptions in your life or detours; deserts of life seem like life itself.

Crossing either type of desert will change you. We are not the same person when the kids leave home as we were in the delivery room. When you finally get back on your feet after a brush with bankruptcy, you aren't the same person who got into trouble with debt. If joining Alcoholics Anonymous or another 12-step program doesn't change you, then you never really committed to the journey. That's why deserts scare us. Deep down inside, a part of us knows that something's going to change and we can never know in advance what it will be. No wonder that we'd rather climb a mountain.

PHOTO: STAN ZIPPAN

A mountain in the Sahara.

The Sahara contains several impressive mountain ranges: the Hoggar, in Algeria; the Tibesti, in Libya and Chad; and the Air, in Niger. Within our deserts of life and change there are always mountains to climb. These are the singular challenges, projects, and dreams that have specific goals—end results that we desire or strive for.

Changing jobs is a mountain, but changing careers is a desert. Having a baby is a mountain, especially for the mom. But raising a child is a desert. Building your dream house is a mountain. Losing your dream house in a divorce is a desert. Beating cancer is like summiting Mount Everest. Living with a chronic or terminal illness is like crossing the Sahara.

Are you climbing a mountain or crossing a desert? Maybe you are doing both at the same time. Treat them differently. Cold, stiff alpine boots will just give you blisters on the hot, drifting sands of change.

N ight had fallen. We could see nothing outside of the small circle of light cast by the glowing embers. It had been almost an hour since the Tuareg had last visited us, and I was beginning to relax a little.The apartment I'd been sharing in Paris now seemed very far away. My home in Toledo, Ohio, was on another planet, another lifetime ago. I was 20 years old, on the verge of manhood, and at a loss for what to do. How on earth had I ended up in the middle of nowhere, in a tribal land where desert clans wrote their own laws? How was I going to get out of there?

"Hey Donahue!" Tallis called.

I looked over to him and saw that we weren't alone. The Tuareg had returned. He stood still, without speaking. I became uneasy with the silence, so I asked him what he wanted.

"Qu'est-ce que vous voulez?"

"Venez avec moi," he responded.

I couldn't tell if his words were a command or an invitation. He wanted us to come with him. My dry mouth and pounding heart prevented me from speaking. I imagined the rest of his clan waiting for us on the other side of the sand dune with their knives drawn. Was this a trap—an ambush enacted upon hapless travelers in the empty, lawless realm of the desert? Without waiting for our reply, he turned around. A few steps, and the black desert night closed around him. Should we follow him into the darkness?

There are times when something calls to us—invites or commands us—to step away from our campfire to cross the shifting sands of change. Of course we want to huddle even closer to the warmth of what we know and where we feel safe.

At the very least we'd like to have a goal to head toward or a map to follow on this journey. And yet the deserts of change, like my journey across the Sahara, can be an exhilarating adventure in aliveness if we know how to travel. If we allow our deserts to change us, to open us up, to teach us who we are and how to live in the moment, then nothing can match life and its deserts for excitement, fulfillment, and meaning.

What follows are six essential rules of desert travel. As you will discover, these rules are quite different from the practices of a goal-oriented, mountain-climbing approach to life. For example, there is no specific order to the desert rules, so don't try to find one. On any given day or during a certain phase of your desert crossing, some rules will be more important than others. "Follow a compass, not a map," the first rule I describe, is often the last piece of the puzzle for many travelers. "Don't stop at false borders," the last rule in this book, is just as easily encountered at the beginning of a desert as at the end. Enjoy the story in its chronological order. Apply the desert rules as you need them, in whatever order makes the most sense to you at that time.

Chapter One

Follow a Compass, Not a Map

I had spent the night studying my map—
but uselessly, since I did not know my position.
—Antoine de Saint Exupéry, "Prisoner of the
Sand," *Wind, Sand and Stars*

I met Tallis in October of 1976. I had hitchhiked from my home in Toledo to Montreal to board the M/S *Aleksandr Pushkin,* a Soviet passenger liner, for its last transatlantic crossing of the season. I was 20; he was 26. Our friendship was sealed on the third night at sea in the ship's cabaret. We found ourselves screaming into a microphone our rendition of the Beatles' "I Saw Her Standing There." It was the only rock-and-roll number the Russian band could play, and a much-anticipated break from the dreary Slavic folk songs that made up its repertoire. But the band didn't know the lyrics, so Tallis and I became a nightly version of Lennon and McCartney—which quickly lost its appeal for the rest of the passengers.

When we arrived in Europe, we rented a dingy, unheated apartment in Paris with another young Canadian a few blocks from the Bastille. Soon the weather turned cold, wet, and gray, much to Tallis's dismay, for he hated winter—February, to be exact. He absolutely loathed every one of those 28 days. He was the only person I'd ever met whose sworn enemy was a page on the calendar. His goal was to spend an entire February on a tropical beach and escape the sting of the Canadian winters he'd suffered on the shores of Lake Ontario.

Paris in November wasn't much of an improvement over Toronto in February, as far as Tallis was concerned. We were spending most of our time and money in cafés trying to keep warm.

"Would you prefer Cannes or Saint-Tropez? Or perhaps Nice or Monte Carlo?" Tallis chirped to me as I sipped my espresso. His good humor had returned since I agreed to spend the winter with him on the French Riviera. He spread a map of France on the small round café table.

"Where are the topless beaches?" I asked, pretending to be only mildly interested in his response.

I noticed the man at the next table smiling at us. He was in his 60s and well dressed, with a hat and cane. He leaned over with a slightly bemused look on his face.

"Pardon, Monsieur—I hope that I am not impolite, but I couldn't help hearing your conversation," he said with a soothing Parisian accent that sounded like Maurice Chevalier's. "The south of France has beautiful beaches with beautiful women, but in the winter you will see neither of these delights."

Tallis looked up from the map, his finger still firmly planted on the Mediterranean coast. "Why do you say that?" he asked.

"Because the Riviera is horrible in winter. The wind, it is

called *le mistral;* it blows down from the Alps. The south of France is frightfully cold—worse than Paris."

"Where could we find beaches that are warm all winter?" Tallis asked.

"What you are looking for is not on your map, I'm afraid," he said in an authoritative tone.

Tallis looked dumbfounded. I felt lost. We both sat in stunned silence. A sudden dread of spending winter in a grimy little apartment and smoky cafés crept over me. Tallis's aversion to the cold must have been contagious. I didn't want to be in Paris any more than he did.

"So what should we do?" I asked Tallis.

"The answer is very simple," the Frenchman interjected. "You must head south—keep heading south."

"Do you mean North Africa?" I asked.

"If you want to be sure of tropical weather, one must go to the tropics, non?"

"But that means we'd have to cross the Sahara Desert!" I blurted out.

"Air France can fly you to the Ivory Coast in a few short hours," he responded.

"We have very little money," said Tallis. "Even train tickets are too expensive."

"Then you must simply head south," he advised, "by whatever means you can afford."

On a map, the mountain peaks have names but individual sand dunes don't. If you named a sand dune, the map would be out of date before the ink was dry. Yet we often start crossing our deserts of life with maps and itineraries. You probably started your marriage or your career with a map. But the sands have shifted, the map is outdated, and you may be lost. The realization that where we are going is not on our map is for many of us the beginning of our journey.

Is there a clearly marked road to follow across the desert of midlife? Can you know in advance how you'll get through raising teenagers and experiencing menopause at the same time? When the doctor says that the test results are not good or when your marriage is crashing against the rocks, is there an itinerary you can download from the Internet to guide you step-by-step over any of those shifting sands? Not having a map doesn't prevent us from traveling. It only means that we must follow our inner compass.

Whether we are crossing a desert of life or a desert of change, a compass heading should do three things:

1   Guide us when we're lost.
2   Take us deeper into our desert.
3   Keep us focused on the journey rather than the destination.

When my marriage ended, I had no plan for my life. "Now what?" was the question I kept asking myself. The one thing that really mattered to me was my kids, who were 10 and 13. I decided that I was going to have a better relationship with them than I had when we all lived together in the same house. That became my compass heading.

Then the kids moved with their mom from our home in the Selkirk Mountains of British Columbia to Vancouver Island—a nine-hour drive and two-hour ferry ride away. I considered moving to be near them, but there was no guarantee that my ex-wife would stay there, as she was looking for work. I didn't know what to do. I was lost.

So I turned to my inner compass for guidance. That direction—having a better relationship with my son and daughter—helped me decide what to do. For the next 18 months I commuted to the coast to live with my kids for 10 days every month. I rented an efficiency hotel room, and for those 10 days I cooked and they did chores; I drove them to school and watched their soccer games.

When we'd check into a hotel, we would ask how far apart the beds were. If the front desk clerk couldn't guess that we intended to jump from one bed to the other in a variety of Olympic poses, then the complaints from the tourists and businessmen in adjoining rooms soon revealed our activities. We had so much fun that we were actually thrown out of one hotel. This is a very bonding experience between a parent and children who are 10 and 13! That week and a half in a hotel each month brought me closer to my kids and deeper into my desert of parenting.

The third function of a compass heading is to help us pay more attention to our journey. We often avoid the present because it's painful or boring, or we're thinking of our destination. But the right kind of direction makes the present meaningful. The right compass heading makes the sand dune beneath our feet more interesting than the horizon and more real than the mountaintop. Spending 10 days a month on the coast allowed me to experience the everydayness of parenting. All that mattered was that we were together every day; I was a dad and we were a family.

It is more meaningful to follow a compass than a map.

But it can take hard work to find the right direction. Our compass heading is like a personal mission statement about something that really matters. It should describe a way of being or way of living rather than a goal or destination. The direction we follow across a desert of life should be one that has deep meaning and clarity.

When you're mountain-focused, what matters most is the last day or last hour of the climb—reaching the summit. If we live a life obsessed with goals, all that matters is the arrival. An inner compass heading keeps us in touch with what really matters every day of our journey.

Raising a rebellious teenager might cause us to focus on a destination such as when she finally moves out or stops driving everyone crazy. But concentrating on the destination could make us lose what really matters more than anything else. We could miss the chance for a lifelong connected relationship with our child by having tuned out of the daily journey because it was so annoying or painful.

A direction can be as simple as "Have fun." When you were a child, that compass heading probably guided most of your waking hours. It was not consciously chosen but seemed to emerge as the right and natural direction to follow. Could this be a direction you need to follow right now?

Directions often have the word *be* or *have* in them: "be true to myself"; "be patient"; "be in the moment"; "have quality time with my loved ones"; "have a positive attitude"; "have faith in God." These are examples of simple but powerful directions that can guide us in the deserts of life and change.

But we might also follow unhealthy directions. We can "be a victim"; "have an ax to grind"; "have a chip on our shoulder." If we look back, we can probably see with the benefit of hindsight that we've followed the wrong direction at times as well.

Let Go of the Destination

There are three techniques that can help you clarify your inner compass. The first is to let go of the destination.

Tallis and I had a clear picture of sandy beaches on the French Riviera, the cobalt blue Mediterranean, cafés along the boardwalk, and Brigitte Bardot cavorting in the waves inviting us to join her. We had a destination and it was on our map. But all of a sudden there was a vacuum. No destination, no goal, no map, no route. In the absence of a specific destination we found our compass direction: head south.

Goals can be a cheap substitute for a sense of direction. It's easier to set a goal, to choose a destination, than it is to find a deep and meaningful direction that will guide us across a desert of life or change. We've been misled into thinking that achieving goals will make us happy. Many Everest climbers spend only 5 or 10 minutes on the summit. They're too tired to savor the moment, and their lives are in danger if they linger. Already there's a new destination; return to high camp before the weather traps them in a deadly blizzard.

For a man in the desert of midlife, buying the perfect motorcycle or finding a girlfriend half his age might provide temporary relief from the feeling of loss or loneliness. But that renewed sense of vitality will pass and he'll just need another mountain to climb.

There are times in life when goals are important—even essential. If you've recently been diagnosed with cancer, you may be focused on winning that battle. Your doctor may have a plan of action. You have a goal, a destination, and a map to regain your health. By all means start climbing toward your objective. But if that summit eludes you and the issue becomes how to live with cancer, then an inner compass will guide you to bring deeper meaning to your life in the time that remains.

Goals can still have a place in our deserts of life. There are mountains in the desert. But they should be markers or indicators that we are following the right compass heading. We need to have a direction first. Start with finding that inner compass to guide you. To do so, you may need to let go of any goals or destinations until your direction becomes clear.

Tallis and I had no idea how to head south. We couldn't afford train tickets, and hitchhiking in France is pretty much impossible without a short skirt and long legs. At the university, we found an index card posted on a kiosk by two Frenchman: Jean-Luc, an engineer in his late 20s, and André, a semiretired dry cleaner in his 50s. They each had a vehicle and were looking for passengers to share costs on their trip to West Africa.

When I first met Jean-Luc, his olive skin, dark hair, and dark eyes convinced me that he was Spanish and maybe even North African. He had been born and raised in Algeria, but his family was French, *pied noir,* which translates as "black foot." This term was used to describe the French citizens who fled Algeria in the 1950s and '60s during the brutal war of independence.

Left to right: Jean-Luc, André, and Tallis in the Atlas Mountains.

Settling primarily in the south of France, they were immigrants in their own ancestral homeland. Many of their families had been in Algeria for a hundred years.

Jean-Luc's love for Algeria and the desert was genuine and as contagious as Tallis's aversion to winter. As he spoke of the stillness of the Sahara and its vast sand seas, I recalled romantic images of *Lawrence of Arabia*. Jean-Luc described the eerie lunar topography of the Hoggar Mountains in the central Sahara and the enigmatic Tuareg nomads, who still lived there. He told me that there were 15,000 perfectly preserved rock paintings on a desert plateau that dated back 8,000 years, depicting a time when the Sahara was a verdant savannah.

The Sahara was no longer a wasteland to cross en route to our beach. The desert itself began to fascinate me more and more. According to Jean-Luc, the farther south we went, the more mysterious and awe-inspiring the journey would become.

It's a good sign when the journey becomes more interesting than the destination. It's also a matter of survival in the Sahara. The hazards from off-road driving force you to look no more than 10 or 20 feet in front of your car. Hidden rocks can snap your axle, and dangerously soft sand can't be seen until you're right on top of it. But if you look down, you'll notice that the desert is changing—the color of the sand, its texture, its firmness.

Mountain climbers spend a lot of their time looking up. Being destination-focused means that we gaze upward or far ahead because the summit, the goal, or our beach is what matters the most. Squinting constantly toward the shimmering desert horizon means that you'll miss the Sahara. Focusing too much on the summit means that you'll miss the mountain. And there is also much to miss in the deserts of life: the journey itself.

As I write, my friend Alonzo's dad is dying of cancer. It struck suddenly, and its progress has been swift. Each Friday evening as their family celebrates another Sabbath dinner, everyone knows how lucky they are to be together. A terminal illness is a harsh but effective teacher of how to live in the moment. It lowers our gaze to the sand beneath our feet. But we don't have to wait until someone we love is dying to learn how to be present with what is happening right now.

Lower Your Gaze

The second technique for finding our inner compass is to lower our gaze. Once we let go of our destination, we bring our attention to the part of the journey that is right in front of us. A compass heading can help us focus on our journey. And focusing on the journey helps us find our compass.

For example, if you're dealing with serious financial hardship, you might have a goal to become debt free. But it could take years to reach that mountaintop, and you could miss a lot of the journey on the way. If you let go of your destination, you might find yourself trying to live each day within your means, spending no more than you earn. That could, in fact, become your compass heading.

Or lowering your gaze to the everydayness of living within your means could reveal a new and deeper compass heading, such as savoring the nonmonetary richness of life. What would it be like if you followed that compass heading? Savoring the nonmonetary richness of life could guide you to nurture your most important relationships, notice the beauty in the world around you, or express the wealth of your own creativity. Although you might still be in debt, with this compass heading you could live a richer life than most millionaires have.

It's not wrong to have goals. The problem is when the entire focus is on the mountaintop. Getting out of debt is pretty important if you're in serious financial hardship. But taking the focus away from the end result allows something new to emerge. If we're not careful, though, all that emerges is a different goal or another plan. So we should direct our attention toward what is right in front of us, as if that were all that mattered. This is a powerful shift in how most of us live, and it can reveal a meaningful compass heading to guide us.

We can practice lowering our gaze even if we are not in a desert of change or searching for our compass heading. What if we lived every day completely attentive to the present moment? What if whatever you were doing—whether ironing shirts, commuting to work, playing catch with your daughter, or cleaning the lint out of the dryer—was all that mattered? You could still have a to-do list, but instead of focusing on getting the next thing done, you would keep your attention on the task at hand. The fullness of the moment would not be lost in the rush for the future. This attention to the present is a desert mind-set and makes our journeys richer. Perhaps this is why the Tuareg language, Tamashek, has no word for tomorrow.

After separating from France, Algeria changed many road signs from French to Arabic as a statement of its independence. So we were lost in the foothills of the Atlas Mountains. Jean-Luc, who professed to know that area like the back of his hand, was poring over a map that was spread on the hood of his car. André peered over his shoulder.

Tallis and I walked along the side of the road. He was enjoying his first cigarette of the morning. André didn't allow smoking in his little Citroën truck. Jean-Luc was also a non-smoker, which was just fine with me since I was spending 10 hours a day with him in his blue four-door Peugeot sedan. We had found what seemed to be the only two Frenchmen who didn't chain-smoke the sweet black tobacco so popular in France.

Unlike us, they had precise destinations. Jean-Luc was on his way to Nigeria, hoping to work in the oil fields and sock away vast sums of tax-free income. André had taken leave of his dry-cleaning business in Normandy to realize a dream. It had been a goal of his for many years to visit the metaphorical end of the earth, Timbuktu. I was surprised to learn that the place actually existed. Once a thriving cultural, commercial, and Islamic center, it was now a dusty outpost on the southern edge of the Sahara Desert.

I sauntered up behind them as Jean-Luc and André studied their map. Jean-Luc explained that there was only one road they were interested in, the N-1 highway. It was the quickest, most direct route into Algeria's vast Sahara. Forgetting that we were only paying passengers and that the Frenchmen would plot the route, I suggested that we simply keep heading south. Jean-Luc said that would be a waste of time; they didn't want to wander all over northern Algeria.

In a world that values efficiency, wandering has a pretty bad name. But that's only because we apply mountain values to the deserts of change. When I climb the spectacular glacier-capped mountains of British Columbia, I'm looking for the safest, most direct route to the top. I prefer day climbing, so there's only so much time to get up and down before dark. The last thing I want to do on a mountain is start wandering.

In a desert, wandering is efficient if it leads you to a truer sense of direction. In the long run, you'll make better progress if you know what compass heading to follow. In Australian aboriginal cultures, a *walkabout* is a coming-of-age ritual in which a young man wanders alone through the desert to learn more about his own character and strength—a good way of finding what his compass heading in life will be.

Sometimes we have to wander around, get lost, and chase a mirage so that we can home in on our proper direction. As with real compasses, which need to be corrected for deviations in the earth's magnetic field, we have to allow for our inner compass's not always pointing true. We also have to allow for our own inability to read our internal compass. After following directions that parents, bosses, spouses, and society have laid out for us, we may struggle at first to hear the faint whisper of direction from within. Also, if the compass direction we need to follow is unpleasant or painful, we can find lots of reasons to head in the other direction entirely. It takes time to find our bearings.

A natural result of letting go of a destination is the feeling of being lost. Our low tolerance for ambiguity may push us to find a new destination to replace the old one. But we have to resist the urge to impose structure, plans, and goals on our deserts. We might be rewarded with a sense of direction if we can stand the uncertainty. Learning how to wander on purpose is a good way to manage the discomfort of uncertainty.

Wander on Purpose

There are three mistakes people make when they wander. One mistake is to focus on the destination. We search for the perfect job, our soul mate, an instant cure for the emotional pain of childhood, an easy solution for an addiction. Wandering on purpose means that we're looking for direction to guide us, a path to walk—not a magic potion that solves our problems instantly.

Other times we wander around the edges of a desert of change. It's a way of avoiding the journey. We pretend that we're trying to find our direction, but we're really just avoiding the desert. An example might be the professional student who keeps pursuing new degrees or fields of study because he's avoiding the desert of life called "having a career."

The third mistake is to wander unconsciously. This is when we go on autopilot. We stop paying attention to where we are headed and drift off course. We start a job or a relationship with a clear compass heading, but then we lose touch with our direction. We wake up years later to realize that we aren't following our compass or that the direction no longer matters.

In my early 30s I decided to become a stand-up comic. The road to success was pretty well mapped out. You began as an amateur at open-mike nights. After developing seven minutes of solid material, you could find work as an opening act. Eventually you'd be a headliner, once you had 30 to 45 minutes of top-notch comedy; then you'd go to New York, Vegas, and eventually your own sitcom in Hollywood. The road and destination seemed pretty straightforward to me.

My most successful stand-up performance was also my last. I'd been allotted seven minutes at an open-mike night in a comedy club in Toronto, where I lived at the time. I delivered my jokes and no one laughed. Nothing. Not a chuckle. Then I had an idea. I repeated my routine almost verbatim to that very same audience, this time inserting the F-word before each punch line. The audience howled with laughter. In the same seven minutes I'd found out how I could succeed as a comic while discovering it wasn't my new career.

When I let go of the destination, my mountain became a desert. Stand-up comedy was a mirage, not a summit. Instead of climbing the mountain called "becoming a comedian," I started crossing the desert called "changing careers." I didn't know what my next career would be. But I hoped that some direction would emerge.

I lowered my gaze and focused on my current job as a corporate fitness and wellness consultant. Most of my time was spent working with individual employees to develop a fitness and lifestyle regimen. But occasionally I would deliver a sales presentation to a potential corporate client. After one such presentation, I received a standing ovation from the committee I'd spoken to. Amazingly, I didn't get the contract, but I did get a clue to my direction. My compass was pointing toward speaking in public.

Next, I responded to an ad to teach classes for people who wanted to stop smoking. The only two requirements were a desire to speak in public, which I had, and being an ex-smoker, which I wasn't. So I lied. I fooled my employers because they were desperate for seminar leaders. I didn't fool my students. Nicotine withdrawal does two things—it puts you in a bad mood and it gives you X-ray vision. Those smokers saw right through me. They could tell I'd never touched a cigarette in my life. So I quit the job.

But I was wandering on purpose, and my compass heading was becoming clearer. I'd learned even more about my direction by following a second mirage. Not only did I want to speak in public, but I also wanted to speak to audiences that weren't drunk or irritable from nicotine withdrawal. Most important, I wanted to be myself rather than impersonate someone else.

Try following a compass heading for a day or a week. Name a desert you're in, even if it's just the grand desert of life, and choose a direction, a way of being, a way of living. Wander along that path for a while. Keep asking the question, "Is this taking me deeper into my desert?" Ultimately, that is the only way to cross a desert—to go deeper into it. Your compass should help you focus on the journey while heading in a consistent direction that has meaning for you.

There is a verb tense called the *present progressive*. This is a good way to think of our compass. It keeps us in the moment while we journey deeper into our lives. With the right sense of direction, we can make this kind of progress even when we're lost and our maps no longer work.

Chapter Two

Stop at Every Oasis

The more you stop, the farther you go.
—Desert proverb

T allis chose five rocks and took aim. Three of my five shots had already found their mark—another road sign no one could read.

Bang!

"One for one!" he called out.

There was certainly no shortage of stones. The northern Sahara consisted of stones piled in heaps, scattered over high plateaus, stone hills, stone valleys. Everything was ancient rock except for the narrow ribbon of black asphalt that snaked down the leeward side of Algeria's Atlas Mountains. According to Jean-Luc, this was the desert. And he was, after all, the expert.

"Jean-Luc is getting on my nerves," I said.

Tallis drilled the sign with another direct hit. "Two for two."

"I can't stand listening to him all day in the car. He thinks he knows everything. He says this pile of rubble is the desert. This isn't a desert; it's the Flintstones' backyard!"

Tallis, left, and I throwing rocks in the northern Sahara.

Tallis cocked his right arm. "What's it matter to you? At least we're heading south."

"Ha! You missed. You're two for three!"

"Your whining is distracting me," Tallis complained.

"Complain all you want, but if I win, I get your transistor radio," I shot back.

"Yeah, and if I win, I get your sleeping bag."

Bang!

"Three for four—we're tied!" Tallis shouted.

Creature comforts were becoming more important. While the Frenchmen bedded down in their vehicles, we slept outside on army cots. Tallis coveted my thick down sleeping bag for the frigid desert nights. I wanted his radio. He spent hours searching for a shortwave transmission from his beloved Canadian Broadcasting Corporation. I preferred the exotic wailing chants of real Arabic music.

"Allons-y," Jean-Luc called out.

It was time to go. Tallis's rock sailed wide of its target.

"It's a tie. You freeze again tonight!" I taunted him.

We climbed back into the vehicles. André and Tallis led the way in the little Citroën truck. As the road began descending to a plateau, André pulled onto the shoulder and stopped.

"Now what?" I mumbled to myself. Then I saw it: hundreds of thousands of palm trees, vast groves, green geometric swaths blotting the desert below. Closer to us, rising from the baked desert rocks, were the five towns of the M'zab oasis. Five hills, each with a mosque at its pinnacle and a medieval wall encircling the thousand-year-old buildings. André was pointing at one of the hills.

"Voilà Ghardaia," he said.

Our first oasis—the view was breathtaking. I felt like I'd stepped back in time to a story from *A Thousand and One Nights.* I couldn't wait to explore it. Then I looked at my watch; it was 10:30 in the morning. We'd only been driving a couple of hours.

I asked Jean-Luc and André if we were going to stop at Ghardaia.

They looked at me the way all Frenchmen look at an American when he says or does something unimaginable. Jean-Luc shook his head and walked back to the Peugeot. André looked at me and spoke solemnly.

"Dans le désert, on s'arrête à chaque oasis." (In the desert, we stop at every oasis.)

The French have perfected that look. It conveys shock, dismay, disapproval—even disgust. The closest North Americans get to that expression is when a cell phone rings at a funeral and your distant cousin who sells time-share condos reaches into the pocket of his shiny suit and takes the call.

It's too bad there isn't someone to give us that same look whenever we consider skipping an oasis. Whether we work through lunch, give up our Saturday morning run, cancel our massage, take our laptop on vacation, or answer the phone during dinner, we are breaking a desert rule: stop at every oasis.

There ought to be a software program for your Palm-Pilot or computer calendar whereby every time you scheduled work on the weekend, a picture of some snooty French person with that expression of dismay would pop up on the screen. Better yet would be that classic image of a bedraggled French Foreign Legionnaire crawling over a sand dune, hoping he'll see an oasis and its life-giving sustenance. That image is actually more appropriate; most of us are like that legionnaire—in desperate need of an oasis.

In the Sahara there are three reasons to stop at an oasis. First, you need to rest and rejuvenate. Second, you must reflect on your journey and make changes if necessary. Finally, at the oasis you can connect with other people who are on the same journey. Everyone knows that we need to take time for ourselves to do the important things, not just the urgent ones. But why don't we stop?

The problem is that we think like mountain climbers. We suffer from *summit fever*. We push just a little harder, hoping we can rest when we get to the top. When we postpone an oasis until our to-do list is finished or until we've answered all of the 193 emails in our in-box, then we have summit fever. Putting off any oasis until the reorganization at work is over, the kids finish school, the divorce is final, or we retire means that we've made the destination our priority. When retirement becomes the great oasis where we make up for all the ones we skipped en route to our summit, we know that we've forgotten this crucial rule of desert travel.

Even mountain climbers know the danger of this mental state. Many climbers on Everest have lost toes and fingers to frostbite, and even their lives, when they pushed for the summit in a state of extreme fatigue. Fortunately, few Saharan travelers suffer from summit fever. That's because there's no summit—just the same distant horizon as the previous day. Desert travelers look no further than the next oasis. By seeing life as a desert and not a mountain, we create a fundamental shift in how we take care of ourselves and our significant relationships.

Strangely enough, stopping to rest and rejuvenate allows us to get more done. It takes four times as long to recover from burnout as it does to prevent it. The desert wisdom at the beginning of this chapter is paradoxical: the more you stop, the farther you go. Nomads remember what we have forgotten—that by stopping more often, we can actually travel deeper into the deserts of life.

Rejuvenation is about more than getting enough sleep. We need time alone, unstructured time, for things like staying in bed and reading the weekend paper from front to back. We need to play, to laugh, to make love, or to drink an exquisite bottle of red wine.

Once upon a time, hanging a sign on your office door that read "Gone fishing" was a legitimate way of announcing that you'd taken the afternoon off work. Now it's just the opposite. We should be hanging a sign on our empty beach towel or those dusty golf clubs that explains our absence from an oasis. The sign might say, "Checking my email."

Unrelenting summit fever drives us to get things done, but the deserts of life and change will exact their toll if we don't stop at every oasis.

A ndré was twirling a dish towel over his head like David taking aim at Goliath. Bits of leafy greens were flying through the air. Tallis and I watched with amusement. He spread the towel on the hood of the Peugeot and said, "Voilà!" There was the result of his afternoon at the oasis: fresh salad, washed and spun dry in the French dish-towel method. He explained that Ghardaia was our last chance to eat fresh greens, and he began concocting a vinaigrette dressing.

Jean-Luc was loading jerry cans of water and gasoline into the space that had previously been the backseat of the Peugeot. Tallis sat down on the discarded car seat and poked at the fire. We were both exhausted from exploring the oasis. After wandering through the maze of Ghardaia's narrow cobblestoned streets, I had talked him into visiting some of the other villages of the M'zab. We trudged through the punishing desert sun from one walled town to the next. However, at

Ghardaia, our first oasis town.

each gate a bearded man in a turban and baggy pants stood up to block our entrance.

The Mozabites fled into the desert 1,000 years ago to escape persecution in the north. To protect and preserve their culture, they closed most of the towns of the M'zab to outsiders. They regarded Tallis and me as barbarians at the gate.

We camped on the roadside about a mile out of the oasis. The sun set quickly, like a flare that had been shot over the horizon. Once dinner was over, the chill of the desert night drove us quickly into our sleeping bags and vehicles. A car full of young men passed by slowly.

"Did you see that car? They've done that a few times," I said to Tallis.

"Done what?"

Before I could answer, they started honking their horn and yelling at us.

"What do you think they're saying?" I asked Tallis as I zipped up my sleeping bag.

"Who knows? Perhaps it's 'Welcome to Algeria,'" he responded sarcastically.

André got out of his truck to see what the commotion was about. The carful of Algerians had turned around and was coming back. I asked the older Frenchman if we were safe. He patted me reassuringly on the shoulder.

"Oui, aucun problème."

Then he climbed back into the truck and I heard him locking the doors. The car slowed down. They turned their headlights off but kept driving slowly past. This time they pointed and laughed at us.

The walls around the oasis towns made a lot of sense to me now. I felt completely exposed and unprotected. These barbarians were invading my oasis of sleep. The car continued up the road with its lights off, and I couldn't tell if it was turning around or continuing on. My ears strained for a sound to indicate what it was doing. Headlights appeared, high beams, and the car roared past us with laughter and loud Arabic music pouring out of it.

The wall around an oasis keeps bandits, barbarians, and nonbelievers at bay. A wall also provides protection from sandstorms. It defines the boundary of your refuge. You feel safer because the wall separates the desert from the oasis.

The digital age has made life easier and safer by eroding many irritating barriers. We can now work from home via fax and the Internet. Our teenagers are never farther away than a cell phone call. Videoconferencing brings meeting participants face-to-face when they're a continent apart. However, we've also lost many of the boundaries that naturally defined and defended our oases. Home-office paperwork spills onto the kitchen table, and the business phone rings at 3 a.m. Cell phones find us on vacation or on the golf course. We've become more accessible to our clients, coworkers, and kids, thanks to the digital revolution. Telemarketers and email spammers know what we buy, when we're home, and how to reach us. "The walls have come down" is a rallying cry of the postmodern world. It's also a lament for a time that was slower and had clearer boundaries between work and rest.

Build a Wall

The single most important thing we can do is to put a wall around our oasis. This can be as simple as unplugging your phone at night. An agreement with family members to enjoy dinner and not answer the phone is a wall. Leaving your laptop at home when you go on vacation is like installing a turbaned guard in baggy pants at the oasis of your summer holidays.

Somewhere along the road to prosperity, we've lost hold of the most powerful two-letter word in the English language: *no.*

"Can you work late?" "Of course!"

"Can you come in on the weekend?" "Absolutely."

No is a wall.

To the Mozabite elder, Tallis and I were easy to identify

as westerners. Even Algerians who are not from the M'zab are evident by their dress or language. But the barbarians who invade our oases can be more difficult to identify. Sometimes they are the people we love the most.

Our children, spouses, partners, parents, friends, and coworkers can be the most persistent invaders. Spouses and partners need time alone, away from each other. A husband and wife need time together away from the kids. Our business colleagues don't need to call us on the weekend. But it's our job to put up the wall. Intending no harm, Tallis and I would have walked unknowingly into the closed towns of the M'zab oasis. But there was a wall, a guard, and a gate.

Sometimes our own thoughts, fears, and mind chatter can be the barbarians invading our oasis. When my son was born, he almost died. He was flown by helicopter to Toronto's Hospital for Sick Children, and his life was saved. But the two weeks spent at his bedside in the neonatal intensive care unit were a desert for his mother and me.

Every couple of hours I would go outside for a short walk. This was my oasis. But as soon as I left the hospital, I began worrying. "What if he dies when I'm away? What if he's had brain damage from lack of oxygen?" Fear and worry were the barbarians that invaded my much-needed oasis. I would return to the hospital more distraught than when I left for my walk.

I decided to have imaginary conversations with him while I walked the downtown streets of Toronto that August. I told him about all the things we'd do together: play catch, go for bike rides, go fishing. My imaginary conversation was a wall that kept the fear away. Gradually I began to notice the vibrant urban life around me. I would watch street performers or walk through the shaded grounds of Queen's Park. Refreshed, I could rejoin my wife in the desert of our bedside vigil.

The next time you go to the bathroom, leave the door unlocked. See how much you enjoy that. No one ever questions the necessity of a latch on that door. It's one of the few oases that still have a wall. Start putting up more walls. It will actually allow you to be more available when you're not at an oasis.

Think of a desert you are crossing. What kind of oasis do you need? Should you be sleeping more? Do you need a massage every week? Should you reflect on your compass heading? Would you like to connect with your kids, your partner, or an old friend?

Next, make a list of the barbarians that could invade your oasis: friends, relatives, colleagues, kids, bosses, clients, commitments, projects, your to-do list, your own perfectionism.

Finally, put a wall around your oasis. Put up a clear boundary that separates desert from oasis. Be prepared. The nonbelievers will test you. We live in a world of nonbelievers—infidels who do not respect the oasis concept. Even parts of us are nonbelievers. We can be our own worst barbarians. Our inability to say no is sneaky. It tricks us into unlocking the gate to our oasis. Our sense of perfection whispers in our ear and promises us a well-deserved break if we put off our oasis until the desert is crossed. Yes, the mountaineer in nomad's clothing can be the most dangerous barbarian of all.

G hardaia is the gateway to Algeria's Sahara. Oncoming traffic all but ceased once we left the oasis of the M'zab behind us. Hours would pass without seeing another vehicle. We drove in silence. Somewhere south of Ghardaia, as our small convoy sped along the single lane of asphalt deeper into the void of the world's greatest desert, I realized that I hated Jean-Luc. I couldn't put my finger on it. There was no single incident or act that caused me to feel the way I did. Maybe we were just too different, or perhaps too similar.

El Golea, the next oasis, was less than a day's drive, but I was already thinking of In Salah, the third oasis. There were rumors that In Salah was infested with malaria-carrying mosquitoes. I was taking my antimalarial medication, but Jean-Luc wasn't. I fought past my increasing dislike of the single-minded engineer to try to convince him to start popping his pills. But it was in vain. He just wouldn't listen to me.

"C'est impossible. Les moustiques n'existent pas dans le désert."

Yes, Jean-Luc was the expert, not only about the desert but about malaria as well. He'd previously contracted the disease in equatorial Africa. According to Jean-Luc, there was no need to take the antimalarial medicine until we crossed the Sahara. According to my guidebook, having been previously infected, he was at even greater risk.

We arrived at El Golea in the brutal midafternoon heat. It must have been over 100 degrees. And this was January—I couldn't imagine what the summer must be like. No wall around this oasis. The desert seemed to blow right through it. We managed to wake an employee of the only gas station to refuel. Neither Jean-Luc nor André had any interest in stopping for anything other than gasoline and water.

André pointed out a small villa on the edge of town. There was a low wall around the dun-colored buildings. He explained that it was a French Catholic mission. Large deciduous trees offered welcome shade, and the grounds seemed peaceful. I wanted to go there and wander around. I needed to think, to reflect on our situation. I needed to be alone. We seemed to be heading toward disaster. Jean-Luc wasn't taking antimalarial drugs, I hated his guts, and we were not stopping at every oasis.

"On roule!" Jean-Luc called out.

We climbed into the vehicles and headed south toward uncertainty at In Salah.

Another reason to stop at an oasis is to reflect. The calm and tranquillity allow you to look back on the stretch of desert you've recently crossed. If problems have arisen, they can be thought through and remedies implemented. You can also look forward and see if you're heading in the right direction. The reflecting at an oasis is a time to look at the big picture. Many Saharan oases are also intersections of highways or caravan routes. At an oasis we can change direction after we've reflected.

Many of us reflect on our direction in life only when crisis, tragedy, or perhaps a significant birthday forces us to look at the inner compass we've been following. Sometimes we even resist those natural opportunities to review our life and direction. When I turned 29, an older friend of mine said, "Oh boy, next year's the big 3-0! Are you ready for that?" I had never really thought about turning 30, but the more I thought about it, the more daunting it seemed. I started to tell people I was 30 years old. I thought that practicing while I was 29 would give me a year to prepare for the shock and tragedy of getting old. People would ask me how it felt to be the big 3-0. I'd say, "Kind of like 29." When I finally did turn 30, it was a breeze. No sweaty palms, no checking the mirror for signs of aging, and definitely no reflecting.

It worked so well that I tried the same mental trick when I turned 39. After two weeks of lying about my age, I realized that I was a complete moron. In fact, I noticed a yearning to do exactly what I'd avoided 10 years earlier: reflect on my life and on getting older. Not only was I entering my fifth decade, but also we'd just moved our family across the continent, my wife and I were building our dream house while our marriage was falling apart, and my business was nose-diving. I desperately wanted to reflect on my life, take stock of my situation, reassess my direction, and make some changes.

Water What's Dry

One way to decide what type of oasis you require is to water what's dry. If your desert is chaotic, you need to find peace and quiet, meditate, take a yoga class. If you spend all day with small children, your oasis might require adult conversation. If you spend most of your day alone, then getting out for social interaction is an oasis. Peering into a computer screen all day is a digital desert. Sinking your hands into the loamy soil of your flowerbed and admiring the radiance of flowers might be just the oasis you need.

Different deserts require different oases. As my life was falling apart at 39, I needed an oasis of reflection. My inner reflective world was parched. When my friend Pam's husband died suddenly of a heart attack, she became a widow and single mother of four at the age of 45. Her weekly massage became an oasis of physical contact, the water of life in her desert of loss and loneliness.

Don't try to turn your entire desert into a lush garden. If your husband just died, then grief and loneliness are part of your desert. But brief respites, whether a massage or a chat with a dear old friend, can sprinkle a little water onto the dust.

I read an article about a funeral director who worked as a clown on weekends. If your desert is serious, you need to have fun. Many of those nasty-looking leather-clad bikers on Harley-Davidson motorcycles are accountants, actuaries, and high school vice principals. If you spend all day following or enforcing rules, then your oasis might be about rebelling.

Many of us have to be nice all day long. It's called *customer service*. To water what's dry means that we need an oasis where we can get even! Maybe that's slamming a volleyball or annihilating an opponent in a squash match. It might be as simple as destroying an ancient civilization in a video game. A desert is defined by its lack of water. Notice what is dry, what is missing in your life. Use that as a guide to what kind of oasis you need.

I watched Tallis trudging back to our campsite on the edge of In Salah, his camera bag slung over his shoulder. He was returning from shooting pictures of the massive dunes encroaching on the oasis.

"Did you get any good shots?" I asked.

"Yeah, the late afternoon sun was at the perfect angle. How's Jean-Luc doing?"

"Not well. André says his fever keeps climbing," I replied. "He says it's almost 40. But I'm not sure what that means in Fahrenheit."

"He must be at 102 or 103; that's not good," Tallis said gloomily.

Nothing had been good since we arrived at In Salah. The place was a fetid, swampy desert junction swarming with mosquitoes. The stillness of the evening brought a pestilence of buzzing deadly vectors. Jean-Luc was delirious with some kind of fever—probably a malarial relapse.

"I wish he would've listened to me. That guy is so stubborn, such a know-it-all. And now look what's happened," I complained.

Tallis nodded but kept quiet. I got up and walked toward the dunes to reflect on our situation. I realized that not long after we left Paris, I'd decided that Jean-Luc was a typical arrogant Frenchman. I'd made no real effort to get to know him. Perhaps he'd have listened to me if I'd been able to connect with him on a personal level. I started to think about André. He seemed aloof and unapproachable. I found it hard to talk to him.

When I got back to the campsite, I saw that Tallis had started a fire. A light breeze encouraged the flames and meant that the mosquito assault would be seriously diminished.

At the oasis you can connect with other travelers.

Perhaps our luck had changed. André emerged from the palm-thatched hut we'd rented for Jean-Luc. He was smiling.

"Sa fièvre est tombée."

What great news! Jean-Luc's fever had broken. Dinner was livelier than any meal we'd shared before. We all realized that we'd dodged a bullet. When the time was right, I wanted to connect with Jean-Luc; but what about the other Frenchman? I wondered how I could relate to this man who was older than my father. I asked him what he was like when he was my age.

"Que faisiez-vous à mon âge?"

He paused and looked us over. He seemed to be considering something. The fire illuminated his strong Gallic face and swept-back hair. For the next hour he described his early 20s in Normandy as a member of the French Resistance in World War II. His parents never knew what he did. He kept it secret to protect them. While they slept, he blew up German munitions dumps, searched for downed Allied pilots, and radioed British intelligence. They thought he was lazy, since he slept late every morning.

"Can't judge a book by its cover," Tallis whispered to me, smiling.

He was right. I had thought André was some old fart from Normandy who pressed pants. I was glad we had connected; I was relieved that Jean-Luc would recover. When it was time to go to sleep, André grabbed a shovel and scooped the hot embers from the dwindling fire and spread them on the sand under our cots to warm our backsides. I settled into my sleeping bag as the glowing coals chased away the chill of the desert night.

"Bonne nuit, mes amis," André called to us as he climbed into his truck.

It was the first time he had called us his friends. How things had turned around! I'd never expected this kind of oasis.

The third reason to stop at an oasis is to connect with fellow travelers. When you're driving in open desert, your attention is commanded by the numerous hazards. Even the long stretches of paved road make real conversation difficult. The silence and vastness of desert terrain lull you into a kind of trance. The Sahara becomes a solitary experience even though you're sitting a couple of feet away from someone. Only in the walled-in safety of an oasis can you truly connect with fellow travelers. Aside from making the journey more pleasant, the quality of your relationships can be a matter of life and death.

There's a scene in the movie *About Schimdt* where a recently retired Jack Nicholson looks at his wife of 42 years, snoring in the bed next to him, and wonders, "Who is this old woman who lives in my house?" They have become strangers. The long deserts of life, career, and family can put us into a kind of trance, and we don't connect with those who matter most to us.

Trying to cope in a desert of change takes so much of our time and energy that we can gradually disconnect from spouses, lovers, colleagues, and kids. The dunes of job loss or divorce, the searching of midlife, the financial concerns or radical adjustments of retirement, are liable to make us withdraw from connecting with others so that we can deal with our desert.

Once again, misplaced summit fever causes us to put off the important oases of connecting because we think we'll have more time once the job, project, merger, to-do list, is done. But deserts go on and on, and by the time we make it to the other side, we might leave a trail of discarded relationships. If you're in a desert, the oasis comes first. And one of the things we must do at an oasis is connect.

The Michelin map of the Sahara shows all the major oasis towns, such as Ghardaia, Tamanrasset, and Timbuktu. It also marks small, remote wells, often no more than a hole in the ground with a bucket on a rope. It's good to plan ahead for an oasis that's clearly marked.

When my son was 11, he came home with a notice from the school nurse announcing a course titled "Studies in Healthy Sexuality." Parents were encouraged to begin discussing the facts of life in advance of the formal instruction at school. I read an article about a father who had used this potentially awkward moment to become closer to his son. I realized that this was an excellent opportunity for us to connect. This oasis was on the map. The dad in the article had found it, and so would I. We got a book at the library.

We sat down one Saturday afternoon to find this special oasis. Chapter 1 contained everything I knew about sex, and then some. But there were 17 more chapters. When we were finished, we were both stunned. No connecting, just silence. We went for a walk through a park. Finally my son stopped, looked up at me, and said, "Dad, what's love?"

I thought to myself, "Oh my goodness, this is it! What a question! We've found the oasis, that little dot on the map. We are going to connect!" As I searched my mind for just the right definition of this deep and mysterious human experience called love, he looked over at the tennis court we had just passed and said, "You know, when they say 'love-30,' what's that mean?"

We can miss an oasis even with the best plan and intentions. But those industrious French cartographers haven't found every spring or well in the Sahara. Some of them are unmarked. Even though we may miss what we were aiming for, sometimes we happen upon an unmarked oasis. A chance encounter with a nomad may lead to one of those little treasures. Some are hidden springs that offer ice-cold, naturally effervescent water.

Look for Unmarked Oases

Like those secret desert wells, some of life's sweetest oases are unmarked and unexpected. We stumble upon them, and the trick is to know one when we see it. While it's critical that we plan and schedule our oases in the deserts of life, we don't want to overlook the serendipitous moments of rejuvenation, reflection, or connection.

When my son was 13, he would still occasionally hold my hand. I'm sure he didn't even realize when he was doing it. We'd park the car and walk toward the grocery store, and he'd grab my hand as he'd done when he was a little boy. I certainly never pointed it out. I knew that if I said, "Hey, son, we're having an unmarked oasis of connecting right now," it would be the last time. But I paid attention. I enjoyed it, not knowing when or if it would happen again.

The desert of terminal illness offers a powerful incentive to be open and real with those we love. But the oases of connecting in this kind of desert are often unmarked. You don't know when they'll happen. The imminence of death can cause some people to deny it, and others to focus on practical aspects of wills and health care. You don't know when the connecting will happen. But you have to be ready. It would be a shame to miss such an opportunity.

Unmarked oases come in many flavors; they're not just about connecting. An article in the newspaper can cause us to reflect. A delay at the airport can provide a chance to get a 20-minute treatment at one of those massage kiosks.

The deserts we're crossing can blind us to the unmarked oases. In a desert of grief, who looks for laughter? Yet those two opposing states often abide very close to one another. In the desert of starting a new business, vacations are usually sacrificed in the first year or two. But when an invitation to your 25th high school reunion appears in the mail, maybe it's time to go back home and forget about the business for a couple of days.

When we think like mountain climbers, we often mis-understand an unmarked oasis. It appears as an interruption, a delay, an obstacle in our way to the summit. So we ignore it or remove it. Now that you're starting to think more like a nomad, ask yourself if an interruption might be an unmarked oasis.

Even when we shift from the mountaineering mentality to the desert metaphor, our lives can become dominated by the very desert we're crossing. It's all we think about. An oasis is a break from the desert. Taking a break from the desert makes the desert itself more meaningful.

Any oasis, whether we are resting, reflecting, or connecting, is a chance to practice being in the moment. Many of the most important, meaningful, and pleasurable moments of life happen at an oasis. By their very nature these experiences absorb us so fully that we are not thinking about some distant goal or destination. An oasis is where we practice being fully present. Gradually, we can take that attention into the desert as we journey onward.

Chapter Three

When You're Stuck, Deflate

Don't be so humble—you're not that great.
—Golda Meir

As we sped along the fresh asphalt south of In Salah, I wondered whether Jean-Luc's brush with death had changed him. I hoped he had been humbled by the experience. After all, I'd been right all along. He should have taken his medicine.

Jean-Luc downshifted as we approached some heavy equipment blocking the highway. An Algerian soldier waved us around the trucks and bulldozers. Jean-Luc muttered a disparaging comment about the Algerian engineers, because they appeared to be repairing a road that wasn't more than six months old. All of a sudden, he pounded the dashboard with his fist and shouted, "Merde!"

I looked up and saw the cause of his outburst. "Shit!"

Our mutual dismay seemed to be the first time we agreed on anything. This was not a maintenance crew. They were the road builders. The pavement had ended. Sooner than anyone had expected, the familiar black asphalt ceased.

André, Jean-Luc, and the Peugeot in the feche-feche.

We stared in silence at the sudden arrival of *le désert absolu.* Crisscrossing rutted tracks led in several directions from the road into the sand and rock of the Sahara. André and Tallis pulled up behind us. I could hear similar exclamations of disappointment as Jean-Luc went back to the Citroën to plan the initial off-road route.

We led the way in the Peugeot. Jean-Luc headed east toward a flat plain that was perhaps an ancient lake bed. As we hit the pristine lake bed, clouds of yellow dust exploded from the tires and Jean-Luc shouted again.

"Merde! C'est le feche-feche."

I'd heard about the *feche-feche.* It was soft powdery sand that was a nightmare to drive across. The Peugeot was bogging down as Jean-Luc rapidly changed gears, pumping the clutch and gas like a Formula One driver. But he couldn't maintain forward movement, and the sedan shuddered to a halt. We were stuck.

When the paved road ends, the desert really begins. Up to that point it's difficult to get stuck or lost. This is when the Sahara as well as the deserts of life become challenging. We can speed along the single lane of pavement oblivious to the desert we're crossing. When our life comes to a shuddering halt, we start to pay more attention to the journey, and specifically to our sudden lack of progress. We get stuck in a desert of change because our techniques for driving on solid ground don't work in the soft sand of transition.

Sometimes our pavement ends in a flash, in a heartbeat, in a phone call or email. Our spouse dies of a heart attack at 39; we lose our job without warning; we come home from work to find that the house is empty, with only a note on the fridge explaining what happened.

Shortly after his 45th birthday, my best friend called to tell me that he'd been diagnosed with cancer. The paved road of our relationship and the paved road of his career and day-to-day life ended abruptly. Steve T. got stuck right away. Like many cancer patients, he found it difficult to ask for help.

More often the process is gradual. Sand begins to cover the highway of our career or marriage. The pavement of predictability starts breaking up at midlife, and we are forced to detour into the dunes for greater distances around the crumbling road we've been traveling. Whether it is an abrupt ending or a progressive disintegration of the highway, the result is the same. Eventually we get stuck in the shifting sands of change.

Getting stuck is a precious opportunity to change and go deeper into life. If we never got stuck, we might never realize where we are. Lots of good things can happen from being stuck. But first we have to get better at noticing when we aren't moving.

Know When You're Stuck

When the passion goes out of a relationship, career, or hobby, we might be in a rut. If we don't like where we are but feel that we can't change it, then our rut is deep. Being in a rut feels flat, boring, and uninteresting. This is one sign of being stuck.

A stalemate has that sense of locking horns. People or groups stake out their positions and don't budge. We can even have a stalemate within ourselves. We might want to try something new or take a risk, but our fears or pragmatism prevent us from acting. In a stalemate we feel frustrated or angry.

Feeling trapped is like being between a rock and a hard place. We feel helpless, stymied, and out of options. When Steve T. started treatment for his cancer, he felt trapped between the overwhelming demands of his illness and his difficulty with asking for help.

Having a sense of direction helps us know when we are stuck. The clearer our compass heading, the more obvious it is when we are not moving in that direction. Imagine if your career compass were "I want to have fun doing work that is interesting." It would be much easier to notice when you were in a rut with such a clear direction. Warning buzzers would go off in your head as soon as you felt even slightly bored.

A compass heading for a relationship like "Being more open, up front, and accepting with my partner" would quickly signal when you were stuck. A stalemate wouldn't last too long before you realized you were bogged down in conflict.

If you have a clear sense of direction, then refer to your compass. Lower your gaze to your life. Look at the sand beneath your feet. Are you moving in the direction of your compass or are you stuck? If you do not have a clear compass heading to follow, there is some good news. One of the gifts of being stuck is that it can help clarify what's really important to us. It can help us find our direction.

Another clue to knowing you're stuck is that whatever used to work for you doesn't work anymore. Habits, attitudes, actions, and beliefs that previously produced the desired results have lost their effectiveness. Your charm may no longer win over colleagues at work. Your teenager doesn't respond to threats of punishment as she did when she was younger. Your moodiness or depression doesn't lift as quickly when you go shopping, have a drink, eat a pizza, or have sex. When our success strategies fail us, we initially think we're just having a bad day. But it might be a sign that we've left the paved road and gotten stuck in the feche-feche of change.

André and Tallis had veered to the right to avoid our dust cloud and stopped on a hill. They walked over to us. Jean-Luc was already cleaning sand away from the undercarriage. The midmorning sun was broiling hot, and his T-shirt was soaked.

Without waiting for instructions, I hopped out of the car. Tallis was already at the back of the vehicle. André joined us as Jean-Luc climbed back into the car.

"Un, deux, trois!" he counted and gunned the engine. We leaned into the car and pushed with all our combined strength. Jean-Luc pressed the accelerator to the floor, and the rear wheels spewed the powdery sand out the back of the car, but the Peugeot didn't budge.

André wanted Jean-Luc to let some air out of the tires. This would create a larger surface area as the tire flattened out. Pushing was getting us nowhere. Jean-Luc's heavy foot on the gas pedal had only dug the rear wheels deeper into the feche-feche. The three of us were now covered in the fine powder excavated by the spinning wheels. Tallis and I sat down in the sand a short distance from the car.

"Why doesn't he listen to André? He's an engineer, for crying out loud. He should understand the physics of deflating the tires," I complained bitterly.

"Don't push him," Tallis cautioned. "He likes to be right. Remember, the more you nagged him about the antimalarial pills, the more he ignored you."

"Yeah, but he nearly died! He should listen to somebody for a change."

Jean-Luc began jacking up the rear wheels. André came over to join us. He seemed resigned to let the younger Frenchman attempt his own sand recovery. Once the car's back end was raised, Jean-Luc pushed sand under the tires and released the jack. The undercarriage was no longer scraping on the powdery lake bed.

"Allez-y, nous allons pousser encore une fois."

It was time to push again. André shook his head and slowly rose to his feet. Tallis and I walked over and put our shoulders to the back of the dust-covered sedan.

Jean-Luc stepped on the gas, we gave a shove, and the car lurched forward. He pumped his fist triumphantly in the air as the Peugeot fishtailed forward, spewing more dust over us. It squirmed ahead about 30 yards and started to bog down. One more burst of acceleration buried the Peugeot in sand up to the tops of the wheel wells. Stuck again, worse than the first time.

While climbing Mount Brennan in the rugged British Columbia interior a few years ago, I was struggling to catch my breath a couple of thousand feet below the summit. I asked Bobby, my climbing buddy, at what altitude you start to notice less oxygen. He said, "About 7,800 feet." Then I asked him how high we were, and he took out his topographical map. "About 7,800 feet." I just kept pushing myself up the mountain, struggling for breath, until there was nowhere to go but down. I'd climbed over a vertical mile from the trailhead to the peak. Part of what I love about climbing mountains is pushing myself beyond my normal level of exertion to reach a world of quiet and expansiveness at the summit. Pushing can take you a long way up a mountain.

Sometimes in the Sahara, when a car is stuck, a little shove is all that's necessary to get moving. Other times, no amount of pushing will help. Pushing can make things worse. You push on the gas pedal and the wheels dig even deeper into the sand. When we push in life, it means that we keep trying what has worked in the past. We exert our will, try harder, pressure ourselves or others.

If we're naturally inclined toward problem solving, then that is how we'll cross our deserts. We'll push the vehicle that has gotten us this far. We'll try to figure our own way out of every dilemma. If controlling others or controlling our situation has succeeded before, we'll try that again. In the chaos of a corporate merger or reorganization, we will exert more effort to manage the uncertainty, try to cover all the bases, cover our backside, and plan for every contingency.

I once saw a cartoon that read, "Always bend your knees when banging your head against the wall." Pushing, when you're stuck in life, can be like banging your head against the wall. It's futile, and it just makes matters worse. A small adjustment like bending your knees might save your lower back, but you're still banging your head. Nothing new can happen until you stop pushing.

Stop Pushing

When we stop pushing, we are admitting that our plan doesn't work anymore. We admit that we don't have all the answers. Recognizing that we are stuck and that our pushing isn't working are humbling experiences. But this is the beginning of getting unstuck.

You have to figure out what isn't working. It could be just about anything: perfectionism, needing to be in control, needing to be right, doing everything on your own, expecting someone to rescue you, needing to please others, needing to have a plan. Ask yourself, "What is it that used to work but doesn't anymore?" Try to notice which part of your dilemma feels like banging your head against the wall.

In the desert of becoming an author I got off to a quick start. It took less than a month to find an excellent literary agent who loved my idea. "Gee, this is going well!" I thought as I sped along the single lane of asphalt. Then I hit the feche-feche. I became stuck early in the process of writing a proposal for my book. The chapter summaries should have been a few paragraphs each but were several pages long. They were almost as long as the actual chapters. I needed an editor.

Perfectionism has served me well in the past. "If you want a job done right, then do it yourself" has been one of my mottoes. The idea of inviting someone to hack away at the jungle of words in my proposal was anathema to me. My ego insisted that I could do it myself. I began editing the chapter summaries on my own. They actually got bigger. I kept pushing. The pages kept multiplying instead of shrinking. My book proposal was as long as the book. That was my version of bending my knees. I was still banging my head against the wall. I had the right idea but the wrong editor.

My plan wasn't working. Strategies that had always served me well were only making matters worse. To cross a desert, we must find new ways to travel. But the old ways have to end before we can find new modes of transportation.

Once we stop pushing, stop banging our head against the wall, we have to just hang out in that place of feeling stuck. If you are stuck, don't jump at the first idea or alternative that pops into your head. Just be there in that stuckness for a while. Our natural reaction is to chase after the first idea that can relieve our discomfort. It is a new place to be, an in-between place. Pause there for a while in the space between knowing what isn't working and not yet knowing how to get unstuck.

N o one moved to assist Jean-Luc. We just sat there, stuck. The sun was oppressive. We were exhausted and dirty with dust and sweat. Jean-Luc struggled to get out of the car, but the sand blocked the bottom of the door. He finally forced the door open enough to squeeze out. After surveying the situation, he began unloading sand traction plates from the roof. I could see what was happening. He'd place the steel plates under the wheels for traction and we'd push again.

André marched forward assertively. He emphatically stressed the need to deflate the tires. Jean-Luc countered that the washboard road, once we found it, would batter the car to pieces if the tires were underinflated. André played his trump card.

"Non, on ne va plus pousser."

I agreed with André's ultimatum. I wasn't going to push anymore, either. Jean-Luc said nothing. He started digging around the wheels and under the vehicle. I felt sorry for him. I had no intention of pushing, but I started to dig. Tallis joined in. After holding out a few more minutes, André was clearing sand from the rear wheels. Jean-Luc positioned the sand plates in front of each tire. We sat down to watch. He climbed into the car but didn't' start the engine. He sat there for a couple of minutes. Then he got out, went to the front of the vehicle, and knelt down. A loud hissing came from the Peugeot. André smiled. Jean-Luc was letting air out of the tires.

He climbed back in the car, started the engine, shifted into second gear, and let out the clutch. The car gripped the traction plates and crawled onto the sand. It rolled steadily forward as he gradually increased the speed. The vehicle was free. We were moving again.

At the top of Mount Everest there is only a third of the oxygen that is present at sea level. Those climbing above 26,000 feet enter the "death zone," where brain cells deteriorate rapidly in the thin atmosphere. Most climbers require supplemental oxygen to reach the summit.

Summiting the world's highest mountains requires more than just cans of pressurized air. There's an emotional pumping up that's required as well. Even the metaphorical mountains of life—our goals, our projects, our challenges—often require getting pumped up, psyched up, fired up, so that we can make it to the top.

But in the Sahara the problem is an excess of air pressure, not a shortage. Overinflated tires churn into the sand until even four-wheel-drive vehicles get hopelessly stuck. Pumping the gas pedal only digs you in deeper.

The Sahara has its own death zone. It begins where the road ends. The physical exertion required to clear sand and push your Land Rover in temperatures as high as 125 degrees F can be deadly. People have died of dehydration in as little as 12 hours while trying to free their vehicles.

A part of us may perish in our deserts of change. Our passion, our sincerity, our commitment, can wither and die if we become stuck for too long or push too hard. If we aren't able to let go and change, then our aliveness gets cut off. We don't want to stay stuck for too long in the deserts of life.

When we get stuck, it might mean that our overinflated ego needs a little air let out before we can get moving again. So here is another paradox: letting air out of the tires, lowering the car, actually lifts the vehicle over the sand. We, too, can achieve a tremendous lift from knowing how and when to un-pump our ego. When we let some air out of our ego, we come down to earth and become more human. Before Jean-Luc could decide to let some air out of his precious Michelins, he had to deflate his ego. He had to accept the fact that his plan wasn't working and that his stubbornness was jeopardizing the safety of the group.

I remember a comedy sketch on *Saturday Night Live*, a spoof on motivational speaking. The speaker's best-selling book and sold-out seminars were titled, "You're No Good!" One tearful but newly enlightened customer was interviewed while leaving the seminar. In the testimonial style of infomercials, he looked into the camera and said, "All my life I've been a failure, and now I understand why—it's because 'I'm NO GOOD'!"

I loved this sketch because it spoofed our mountain-climbing mentality, which believes the only way to succeed is by succeeding. We go to great lengths to maintain our edge, our confidence, our ego. It's always about feeling up, feeling good. Mountain-climbing culture makes deflation difficult. Our society loves a winner. We deny weakness and spin any defeat into some inflated version of victory.

In all fairness, it makes sense to believe in ourselves and develop healthy self-esteem. This is especially important when we are young. When my daughter moved to the coast with her mom, she enrolled in the public school system for the first time. Chloé was 13. We quickly discovered that she had an abundance of athletic talent, and she earned dozens of ribbons playing on several school teams. It was a great boost to her self-esteem in a difficult year. When she returned to spend the summer with me in the mountains, I noticed that she had brought her ribbons with her. She said, "If anyone makes me feel bad about myself, I'll just look at these and feel better."

The last thing a young person needs to hear is, "You're no good." Kids are natural mountain climbers, and we should encourage them to set goals, help them to achieve their goals, and build their self-esteem. This is the work of youth and to some degree the work of the first half of life. In a sense, we are building a strong ego (which is not the same as a big ego) so that it can withstand the necessary deflations that are part of crossing our deserts.

The road to success is not paved with success. At times it's not paved at all. The road to a successful life takes us through deserts where we get stuck and what we must do to get moving again is a defeat for our ego. Whether it means admitting that we're wrong, accepting a loss, apologizing, forgiving, asking for help, or acknowledging our weakness, the ego comes out the loser by being deflated.

I had promised my literary agent that she would have my book proposal in two weeks. A month had passed and I was still stuck. Once I stopped pushing, I knew a deflation was right around the corner. I admitted that I needed help and could not do this on my own. So I chose an editor with a reputation for being direct, even blunt, in her criticism;

unflinching in her honesty; and adept at spotting weaknesses in the author's words, vagueness in meaning, and conflicting ideas—I hired my ex-wife. She turned out to be an astute editor. The streamlined proposal worked; it helped me to find an excellent publisher.

But there was an unexpected gift. I was amazed at how a structured business arrangement facilitated what had been a difficult aspect of our marriage—criticism. I was able to appreciate how differently our minds worked and see the value of her perceptions. I was now gratefully paying to receive what I'd avoided at all costs when we lived together. Deflations often bring a surprise gift in addition to the hoped-for recovery from the sand that we're stuck in. It's hard for the ego to accept that it doesn't have all the answers. But the answers may not appear until we lower ourselves. The problem is that we often cannot see or imagine what the benefit of the deflation will be until we let that air out of our ego.

Perhaps the biggest deflation of all is coming to grips with our mortality. Death becomes less of a concept and more of a reality. The runaway best seller *Tuesdays with Morrie* chronicles the incredible aliveness of a man who spread immeasurable joy during the last months of his life. Slowly losing control over his bodily functions delivered succeeding blows to his ego. The result was a man who became more human and loving with each letting go. The triumph of spirit rises out of the deflations of our ego.

But how do we usually deflate? Most of us have gotten the whole thing backward. When someone tries to compliment us, we deflect it by saying, "Oh, it was nothing special." We deflate unnecessarily. Then, when we're really stuck in the sand, we make excuses or blame someone else and miss the chance to deflate by pumping up our ego.

Malidoma Somé is a West African author and lecturer with two Ph.D.s. He is from the landlocked sub-Saharan country of Burkina Faso, where his Dagara tribe still practices ritual initiation at significant life stages. When Malidoma was being initiated into elderhood in his early 40s, he returned to his village from his home in North America. He was instructed to sit for two days in the center of the compound formed by the numerous huts. Tribal members took time out during the normal routine of their village life to stop and insult him. They would dredge up any instance from his life that demonstrated a fault or failure and remind him of how he had let everyone down. They accused, berated, and belittled Malidoma. He was not allowed to respond. The Dagara believe in dealing with an overinflated ego in one fell swoop. It's the African version of "You're no good." They believe that elders need to be deflated before they can be trusted with the responsibilities of leadership.

Look for Little Deflations

Since our culture and communities do not know how to ritually deconstruct an overinflated ego in a healthy way, we have to be in charge of our own deflations. It's better to practice little deflations than to look for some grand epiphany of humility. If we get seriously stuck in a desert of change, a big deflation may be in order. Practicing little deflations in our daily life can prepare us for the bigger ones. Anytime we become demanding, angry, impatient, childish, obnoxious, obtuse, or insolent is a chance to let a little air out of our ego, come down to earth, and move in a healthier direction.

It's not about destroying your self-esteem, being hard on yourself, or becoming a complete loser. It's really about acceptance. A deflation is about accepting a small truth about your imperfection or impermanence. To accept ourselves, warts and all, is a deflation that creates a tremendous lift. The changes we make in a desert are sometimes about seeing things differently, not about being different.

Be ruthlessly honest about what is really going on. Admit it when you're wrong. Apologize when you need to. Forgive the guy who cuts you off in traffic. When something doesn't work out the way you intended, rather than get angry or start blaming, just feel the disappointment. Don't try to fix it or change it or find excuses. Just feel the deflation. Take a deep breath and then notice that you're still in one piece. Your ego didn't disappear completely. But you learned that you can tolerate some deflation.

Deflation is part of life. It's not very sexy. You won't get your picture on the front of *People* magazine by letting air out of your ego. But if there were a *Human* magazine, you'd deserve to be on that cover, because every little deflation, along with the big ones, makes us more human, more real, and in fact more alive.

Being able to deflate allows us to wander. We will chase mirages in our deserts. Finding that inner compass is not an exact science. When a direction we follow turns out to be a mirage, that is inevitably deflating. Feel the letdown. Trust that it was good for you. And continue wandering on purpose.

Last summer I realized that I needed a regular weekly oasis that was fun and competitive. Signing up for a mixed adult softball league was easy for me to do. I'd played baseball as a boy and was confident in my abilities. But that was not the case for a woman on our team. Danielle was from Australia. She had never played any form of baseball in her life. She was new in town and thought it would be a good way to have some fun and make new friends.

In her first game she tried to catch a ball with her bare hand and sprained her thumb. She dropped more balls than she caught and ran the bases backward on a couple of occasions. But she was the only player who came to every game and she probably had the most fun. Deflating herself allowed her to stop at a rejuvenating oasis without her self-image interfering.

How many of us are afraid to dance because of our pumped-up ego? We don't want to look inept. Painting lessons, poetry writing, learning a new language, improv acting classes—in fact, all kinds of rejuvenating oases—await us if our ego can tolerate a little less air. Even when we are close to an oasis we can get stuck in the desert because we insist on looking good, on doing it right. Don't let the fear of a little deflation get in the way of experiencing some new kind of oasis.

Little deflations can prepare us for bigger ones. To truly connect with someone, we may have to swallow our pride, apologize, or own up to a lie, mistake, or betrayal. Letting air out of our ego can get us unstuck in the desert of a difficult relationship and create a healing oasis of connecting.

In the Sahara there is no shame in letting air out of your tires. It's part of the journey. There's no shame in the necessary deflations of life. They lift us out of our stuckness and get us moving across our deserts.

Chapter Four

Travel Alone Together

Remember, we're all in this alone.
—Lily Tomlin

D eflating the tires had worked. We crossed the lake bed and put the feche-feche behind us. We also found the track to Tamanrasset, our next oasis. The track, or *piste,* as the French call it, was one of those bone-jarring washboard surfaces that the Sahara is famous for. The trick to driving on the corrugated desert piste is to accelerate. Somewhere around 50 miles an hour your car skims along the tops of the bumps for a relatively smooth ride. There was one problem: we needed fully inflated tires. Our bicycle pump couldn't completely reinflate the Peugeot's tires.

As we bounced along in first gear, every corrugation shook us. The piste was an endless track of miniature speed bumps. The car was shaking so hard that it felt as if the fillings in my teeth were going to fall out. Jean-Luc stopped to check the roof rack. The constant jarring had shaken it loose, and it was about to come crashing down. One bolt was missing, and when André and Tallis arrived, the Frenchmen began improvising a repair.

A small red van stopped beside the Peugeot. The sole occupant was a large bearded man with blond hair and wire-rimmed glasses. He appeared to be in his late 30s or early 40s. He was perspiring heavily and his face was red. He leaned over, rolled down the passenger-side window, and said in a thick German accent, "I see that your Peugeot needs some air in its tires, *ja?* I have a compressor. Shall I inflate them for you?"

Introductions were made, and we learned that Klaus was a plumber from Düsseldorf. His destination was the famed desert hermitage at Assekrem, a half-day's drive east of Tamanrasset into the Hoggar Mountains.

So we became a convoy of three vehicles. It was a delight to speed along the washboard road at 50 miles an hour. The piste opened up at another dry lake. The surface was firmer than feche-feche, but the lake bed was a minefield of small boulders. The little red Renault van was the first to hit one of the rocks. Klaus's tire exploded, and we stopped for half an hour while he changed it. Only a few hundred yards farther, a rock smacked the differential on the Peugeot's rear axle. André, Klaus, Tallis, and I stood in the oppressive afternoon heat for almost an hour, swatting away the ubiquitous flies, and watched as Jean-Luc used discarded tire tread to fasten a protective covering on the dangerously exposed component of the Peugeot's drive train.

André was getting impatient with all the delays. We had no shelter from the sun. The vehicles became solar-fired ovens when they weren't moving. We were consuming more water than we had planned.

He proposed that the other vehicles keep moving and that each driver take care of his own maintenance and sand recovery. The odds were that we'd all get stuck or break down at some point, and there was little reason for everyone to sit around waiting. In the long run it would even out. While one driver was changing a tire, the others would catch up or pass. The lead vehicle, whichever that was, would stop an hour before sunset and make camp as the stragglers caught up. If anyone suffered a serious breakdown and did not arrive at camp, the others would turn around and search for them in the morning.

André was suggesting a type of desert leapfrog approach to driving that would allow us to make swift progress on our own but still be in touch as a convoy. There wasn't a name for this driving technique, so Tallis dubbed it "travel alone together."

In 1953 Sir Edmund Hillary and Tenzing Norgay, as part of a 12-man British expedition, became the first to reach the summit of Mount Everest. In 1980 Reinhold Messner achieved what was thought to be impossible—he climbed Everest alone and without bottled oxygen. On a mountain you're either alone or together.

However, the most effective convoy technique for crossing open desert is to leapfrog: vehicles travel independently within the group. You're not exactly alone but not really together. And yet it seems that you're both at the same time.

"Travel alone together" is paradoxical. But this desert rule works in the Sahara and in our deserts of change because we need support and we need to travel alone. No one can make our journeys for us. We have to do our own work of finding direction, letting go, taking care of ourselves, and battling with our egos. Yet we can't make it alone, either. We need moral support, companionship, guidance, and understanding from others.

It's not a question of balance. There isn't a formula that determines the proportion of time alone and time being supported. Rather, it is a matter of discernment. At any point during our journey we may need support or a solitary experience; we may need both at the same time. The skill to develop is the ability to discern what we need and when we need it.

Don't Do What's "Natural"

Most of us have a preference for being either team players or soloists. We must pay attention because our natural tendency, that which seems easier to do, may not be what is needed. What's "natural" is often what has worked for us as a mountain climber. It's what has helped us to succeed in a culture that rewards mountain-climbing attitudes and behaviors.

If our natural tendency is to go it alone, do it ourselves, then there's a good chance that we need to find support. On the other hand, if what feels most natural is to ask for advice, take a seminar, or join a support group, then the direction to follow may be solitary.

So what is your preference? When the going gets tough, do you prefer to go it alone or to enlist others to help you? We often respond unconsciously, in a knee-jerk fashion, without taking time to consider whether togetherness or aloneness is required. Since deserts are about change, you might need to be doing just the opposite of what feels natural. At any given stage of our journey, the questions to ask are, "Do I need support right now?" and "Is this something I should do alone?"

The desert leapfrog game became a friendly competition. Whenever we were stuck, I was determined to do whatever I could to expedite freeing the Peugeot. I became Jean-Luc's assistant during repairs, slapping tools into his outstretched hand as he called for them from underneath the vehicle.

While changing a tire he began to speak about his childhood in Algiers—carefree summers on the sun-drenched Mediterranean and the heartbreak of leaving North Africa for France. I finally understood Jean-Luc's circumstance. Although he was French, France was not his home. But he was an unwelcome visitor in Algeria, as were all the French in those years following the brutal war of independence.

For the rest of the afternoon, the lead changed hands several times. André's Citroën fared the best, with its high clearance and air-cooled engine. In the late afternoon, he and Tallis found a small outcropping of rocks to break the wind. The Citroën and Renault created two other sides of the campsite. We were the last to arrive, and the sun was almost down. The searing heat of the day had quickly given way to the evening's desert chill, and their small fire was a welcome sight.

We traded stories and congratulated ourselves on the success of traveling alone together. Klaus went over to his truck and returned with a six-pack of cold German beer. He had wrapped a damp towel around the cans and placed them on the roof of his Renault for the last hour of driving. The rapid evaporation had cooled the lager considerably. Klaus was quickly becoming very popular.

He began to talk about his solo journey. Everything had gone smoothly since he had left Düsseldorf—until the paved road ended. He had gotten hopelessly stuck in the dusty quagmire of feche-feche. Klaus had been struggling for an hour to free his vehicle when we came through the lake bed. We never saw him. But he watched us get bogged down, although he didn't ask for help, since he thought he could free himself. However, when we got moving again and Klaus was alone, he began to worry. Fortunately, a Land Rover heading north passed right by him. A helpful trio of fellow Germans used their powerful winch to pull his truck out of a deep rut. Jean-Luc told him that he was very lucky. Klaus agreed.

"*Ja*, I should have asked you to help me. If the Land Rover did not rescue me, I would still be there."

Have you ever been stopped by a couple in a car who need directions? The woman is usually the one who asks, while the man stares silently forward, defeated. I think I understand why men don't like to ask for directions; they believe they can figure it out for themselves. But guys won't hesitate to ask a buddy to help them move. That's because they know they can't carry a refrigerator down two flights of stairs alone; if they could, they would.

Many of us, both men and women, are like that. If we can get out of our dilemma on our own, that's what we'd prefer to do. Even when we realize that we need help, we wait until we're in really big trouble before we seek any assistance. We don't want to admit that we need help. Or we're afraid to show that we don't have our act together, and asking for help seems like a sign of weakness. We're too proud or too uncomfortable to ask. We don't want to put someone on the spot. We don't want to be beholden to another. We don't want to lose control or be humbled. We don't think we deserve to receive support. There are lots of reasons why we go it alone. It may be difficult to ask for support now, but it only gets harder the longer we delay.

We can end up like Klaus in the powdery feche-feche. The four of us could have pushed him out. But his insistence on trying his own sand recovery only dug him in deeper, until it took every ounce of pulling power from the Land Rover's winch to rescue him.

Steve T. was one of those buddies I could count on when I was moving. My best friend had always been the strong one. Though he was a heavy smoker, Steve T. could still run a 10K in less than an hour, even after months of inactivity. He was the cleanup hitter on our men's softball team. Steve once quit smoking cold turkey, started a five-day juice fast, and renovated his apartment on the same weekend. A lifelong bachelor, he was used to taking care of himself. So when he got sick, that's what he tried to do. Steve was a mountain climber who preferred solo ascents. By the time his mountain became a desert, he was desperately in need of support. He didn't know how to ask for help, and I wasn't sure how to offer it.

One hot summer day we met for lunch, not knowing if he would be able to eat anything. I noticed how much weight he'd lost; his trousers were bunched at the waist from the belt being so tightly cinched. Steve told me that his doctor wanted him to attend a cancer support group. I thought it was a great idea and urged him to sign up. But I could see that he wasn't ready for that experience. Then I offered to buy him a pair of pants that fit properly. I figured he'd make up some story about regaining his weight and growing back into all his clothes. But he agreed to let me buy him the pants. I realized that to give support, I had to meet Steve where he was—offer support where he was able to accept it, even if it was only a pair of size-28-waist khaki slacks. I hoped this was the beginning of some traveling together. Perhaps he'd eventually join the support group.

I've discovered that there are support groups for just about any desert you're crossing. There's even a support group for people who've become addicted to attending support groups. It's no accident that so many support systems have evolved. We can't cross our deserts alone. Perhaps you need to join one of these groups. Maybe you simply need someone to clean your house while you recover from your chemotherapy. Or perhaps the only support you require is a friend who will listen to you complain about how tough life has become since you lost your job.

Seek Support Sooner or Risk Rescue Later

According to comedian Jerry Seinfeld, you can measure the size of a favor by the pause that a person takes after he asks you if you'll do him a favor. If it's a short pause, it's a small favor; a long pause, then it's a big favor. The longer we wait to ask for help, the longer that pause is going to be, because the greater our need will have become.

The together component of this desert rule supports our other desert rules. Sometimes we need support so that we can stop at an oasis. Overworked parents need babysitters or relatives to watch the kids so that they can have some free time. When we're stuck, we need a friend or counselor who can help us gently let air out of our ego and apologize, forgive, or let go. A coach, a book, or a support group can help us find the compass heading we need to follow.

There are many reasons to flag down another vehicle in the desert of life. Seeking support saves our emotional and physical reserves for the crucial and essential things we must do on our own. The whole point of support is that it frees you up to do the real work of the journey. No one can cross your desert for you. Only you can connect with your loved ones. You are the only one who can choose the inner compass that will guide you across this desert called life. Only you can forgive a betrayal, accept your mortality, grow up, grieve a loss, or adjust to retirement. What kind of support do you need to move deeper into the heart of your deserts? Don't wait until the support you need becomes a rescue effort. Seek support sooner.

The dark peaks of the Hoggar Mountains to the east announced that Tamanrasset was near. Relieved to be completing this stage, we all knew that the most grueling and dangerous part of our trip awaited us—the journey to the final oasis, Agadez. Across the border and well into Niger, Agadez was the last true oasis before the desert sands would gradually give way to the sub-Saharan lands. There was no road from Tamanrasset to Agadez; we were faced with 500 miles of featureless sand and rock that had claimed the lives of

The Hoggar Mountains, viewed from Assekrem.

hundreds of travelers. Daytime temperatures could climb to 130 degrees F, and blinding sandstorms could rage for days on end. Straying only a few hundred yards from the piste would mean certain death from dehydration if your vehicle broke down.

We drove through the tree-lined streets of Tamanrasset to a campground and secured the last available campsite. Jean-Luc noticed that the oasis seemed unusually busy. We quickly found out why: the border between Algeria and Niger was closed. Many travelers had been turned back at the Nigerien frontier, halfway to Agadez. The Algerian police were no longer allowing vehicles to travel south of Tamanrasset.

There had been an attempted coup in another West African country. Nervous governments in neighboring countries like Niger had slammed the door on foreign visitors. There was no indication of when the border would reopen.

The Frenchmen decided to return to France. André explained that it would be foolish for Tallis and me to continue alone. Our Algerian visas were about to expire; we were running out of money; and even if the border reopened, no one had room for hitchhikers. Vehicles needed every bit of space to carry extra fuel and water for the 500 miles to Agadez.

Tallis made up his mind immediately. He would continue heading south if I went with him. The perfect beach and a February without winter still called to him. But if I chose to turn around, he'd head back to France with me. The decision was mine. I felt utterly alone. I told Klaus how I felt and asked for his advice. He had an unusual suggestion.

"You must come with me, *ja?* I go to visit the hermitage at Assekrem. There you will be truly alone."

It didn't seem that being more alone was the answer to my dilemma. But I took him up on his offer. Tallis stayed at the campground with the Frenchmen, and I headed into the eerie moonscape of the Hoggars' volcanic peaks and crags. As we bounced along deeply rutted mountain roads, Klaus explained the origin of the famed desert hermitage.

Charles de Foucauld had been an officer in the French Army known more for his debauched lifestyle than for any military success. A viscount born to the aristocracy, he lived the high life while posted to Algeria in the late 1800s. But his life abruptly changed when he left the army. He became an ascetic monk devoted to converting the Tuareg nomads to Christianity. He founded this desert retreat on a 9,000-foot-high mountaintop surrounded by the desolate windswept peaks of the Hoggar Mountains. Foucauld did not proselytize but hoped to win converts through his acts of charity and selflessness.

A hermit's hut at Assekrem.

Although he won the Tuaregs' respect and love, he did not
convert a single nomad to Catholicism.

Inspired by the holy man's piety, Klaus had come to the
Sahara to pray. His young wife was slowly dying, and this
seemed like the only thing he could do. He wanted to be alone
so that he could feel closer to God.

We spent a cold night trying to sleep in his tiny truck. At
6 a.m. Klaus woke me and we hiked in silent darkness several
hundred feet up the rocky path to the hermitage. At the large,
flat tabletop summit, a monk in a woolen cap and down jacket
greeted us. He was a member of the Little Brothers of Jesus,
the order that Foucauld created. Klaus wandered off to the
eastern precipice as the horizon began to glow the bluish
green of a robin's egg. I sat down and leaned against a rock to
watch the progression of colors move across the horizon. I sat
alone, awaiting the sunrise that is thought by some to be one

of the most spectacular on earth. In Tamashek, *Assekrem* means "end of the world," and it felt like that. It was quiet. I felt very small, very insignificant, in the enormous desert. I was alone but I wasn't lonely.

The sun appeared like a silent explosion, a slow-motion fireworks display dazzling the volcanic crags of the Hoggar. After a while I stood up, walked to the path, and began descending to Klaus's truck. I'd made my decision. Tallis and I would travel, somehow, to Agadez. I didn't have a logical explanation for my decision or a plan to get to the last oasis. All I knew was that my compass still pointed south.

Famous painters and writers have used apprentices and assistants in the creation of their masterpieces. Whether in underpainting of canvases or researching background for a novel, team efforts have contributed to some of history's greatest works. Yet some critical essence of the work, whether it was the sketch or the characterization, the shading or the plotline, could never be delegated. The artist or author knew, "This part I must do alone."

A great creative talent might intuitively know what part she alone must do. But in the deserts, change seems counterintuitive. Since our ego resists change, it will often steer us away from the work we need to do. It will advise us to avoid or delegate what needs to be done alone, on our own. When I learned that Jean-Luc and André were returning to France, I had to decide whether we would return with them or continue on our own. I wanted to delegate that decision.

When my marriage ended, I moved out of our brand-new 3,000-square-foot dream home overlooking a glacier-fed lake in British Columbia's Selkirk Mountains. I rented a mobile home in a trailer park. I complained a lot about my ex-wife and drank too much. One day, after a heated argument on the phone, she drove to the trailer and banged her car into mine in a fit of anger. I felt as if I was living the lyrics of a bad country-and-western song.

One evening I was feeling sorry for myself and channel surfing when I stopped at a program from the Grand Ole Opry. The show featured past and present stars singing classic country-and-western songs. As I opened a beer, a silver-haired gent in a blue and white cowboy jacket started singing, "I'm So Lonesome I Could Cry." I agreed with him and started crying. I didn't want the song to end. It seemed as if it had been written for me. I reached for a pen to jot down the toll-free number and order my very own video-tape of the program.

When I realized what I was doing, I stopped cold. I'd never phoned an 800 number to order something advertised on TV—not Ginsu knives, not abs-of-titanium contraptions, and certainly not any country-and-western music. I'd either completely lost my mind or had an epiphany.

Somehow that song and my bleak surroundings made me realize how utterly alone I felt. I couldn't avoid or delegate it—I just had to feel it. Then a strange thing happened. When I accepted my aloneness, I felt less alone. How many country-and-western songs have been written about this desert, this loneliness of a broken marriage? Others had walked this path. I suddenly had the company of thousands who were just as alone as I was. I didn't care at the time that most of them probably thought Elvis was still alive. If we can tolerate being alone, support sometimes appears.

Acceptance, even direction, can emerge from within if we can just be with ourselves for a while.

The right kind of support helps us be alone. A terminally ill person can face the aloneness of death with a friend or even a stranger such as a hospice volunteer by her side. The dark or confusing journey of a midlife crisis is more navigable with a skilled therapist, minister, or mentor to assure us that we can find our way. The acid test is in not looking for someone to make our journeys for us. Even with support, we are still alone. Klaus wouldn't make my decision for me. He shared his aloneness with me by taking me to what is possibly the most remote and stunning hermitage in the world. He allowed me to be with myself. If we are truly alone, there's a chance that something will happen; something might change. This is when the quiet certainty of our inner compass might be revealed.

Often in the desert of marriage, we lose ourselves in the other and forget who we are. In the book *The Marriage Sabbatical* Cheryl Jarvis describes middle-aged women who, after decades of caring for children and husbands, take time out from the marriage to pursue an interest or learn more about themselves.

She details the experiences of several women who leave their marriages for a few weeks to as much as two years. One woman goes to a writers' retreat and writes a book; another spends two years in the Peace Corps. Being alone, away from their families, allows something new to come into their lives. They discover and connect with a part of themselves that was invisible amid the day-to-day demands of marriage. But then they return to their relationships and bring back what they have found.

When it's time to be alone, it's better to be like a desert hermit than a solo mountain climber. Alone in a desert, whether it's a real Sahara or a desert of life, we're more likely to hear the whispers of God, our soul's yearning, or the guidance of our own deep wisdom. There isn't a planned route for this kind of communication. There's no goal. There can't be a schedule. We just have to be alone. But being alone isn't about being lonely, because in solitude we can connect with something bigger than ourselves.

Become a Part-Time Hermit

It's important to be a part-time hermit, not a permanent hermit. We don't know exactly what will happen in our alone times. But something happens, something changes— we find our direction, we become rejuvenated, we accept or let go of something. And then we return.

Being a part-time hermit makes it safer for those of us who fear loneliness, because we know it's temporary. Being a part-time hermit helps solo climbers remember to seek support. And if we make it clear that we are only temporary hermits, then it's easier for those who need us—children, spouses, coworkers—to tolerate our emotional or physical absences.

Crossing our deserts of life is a dance between solitude, loneliness, togetherness, and support. Either being alone or being together can be what's required to get us moving again and take us deeper into our desert. If you need more clarification, you can ask, "What will help me get moving again?" or "What will help me find the right compass heading to follow?"

"Is sont absolument fous!" André said to Jean-Luc when I told him we'd decided to continue heading south on our own. He thought we were crazy. It was hard to tell how Jean-Luc felt until he gave me the money.

"C'est pour quoi ça?" I asked.

"C'est pour ton lit de camp, la nourriture et l'essence," he replied.

He wanted to buy my army cot and give me back all the money I had paid for food and gas. I protested. No one owed me a refund. This wasn't a package tour I'd signed up for, and it wasn't anyone's fault that the border was closed. He pretended not to understand my French. I took the money.

"Allons-y," Jean-Luc called to André and Klaus, who were already in their trucks.

André rolled down his window and started driving away. He looked back and shouted at us, "Il ne faut pas s'arrêter à la frontière! C'est dangereux!"

"What did he say?" Tallis asked.

"He said, 'Don't stop at the border. It's dangerous.'"

"What's that supposed to mean?"

"I don't know—I guess we'll find out when we get there. If we get there."

Chapter Five

Step Away from Your Campfire

In a dark time, the eye begins to see.
—Theodore Roethke, "In a Dark Time,"
The Collected Poems of Theodore Roethke

T he Frenchmen's departure left me with a strange mixture of regret, fear, and excitement. I wished I had gotten to know them better, but now they were gone and we were truly alone. It seemed that the journey was just beginning.

Jean-Luc had given us the one thing we needed more than anything else: cold, hard cash. To preserve our precious currency, we decided to camp in open desert several miles outside of the oasis. We hitched a ride with some Swedes who were heading into the Hoggar Mountains and found a flat spot on top of a rocky hill near some dunes.

The Sahara is relatively young as a desert. Spectacular rock paintings by Neolithic hunter-gatherers depict lush grassland 6,000 to 8,000 years ago. A few species of small antelope still remain in parts of Algeria and Niger. Any firewood you stumble upon might be hundreds if not thousands of years old. We spent most of the day scouring the hillside for bits of ancient wood so that we could have a small fire at night.

As dusk approached, the desert seemed to grow more and more immense. I felt incredibly minute, like a flea on an elephant's back—unnoticed, unimportant, at the mercy of my host, taking me wherever it went. The Sahara now owned us.

The first fresh crackles of the fire calmed me. The pale six-foot radius of light and warmth became my refuge from the great, dark unknown of the desert. I knew I could make it through the night if we kept the fire going.

Then the nomad appeared. We gave him our salt and pepper, and then he ordered us to follow him into the desert night, away from our campfire. Was it an ambush? I wondered what the cold steel of a Tuareg dagger might feel like across my throat.

Tallis stood up, ready to follow the Tuareg into the darkness.

"What if there's seven or eight of his clan members waiting for us with their knives drawn?" I hissed through clenched teeth. "I think we should either stay put or get the hell out of here!"

He dusted the grit from his hands and the seat of his pants.

"You're too paranoid," Tallis said. "Where could we go? There's nothing but open desert out there. Besides, these Tuaregs could be testing us. If we haven't got the guts or the good manners to go with him, then maybe their customs dictate they slit our throats while we're sleeping."

With the last sentence, I heard a mocking tone creep into his voice. I flicked my flashlight back on, and my hunting knife glinted in the searching beam.

"Don't even think about taking that knife—or the flashlight, for that matter," Tallis ordered.

"But it's pitch-black out there!"

"Our eyes will adjust once we step away from the fire. Now let's get going, before he disappears over the ridge of the sand dune."

The campfire looked safe and warm. Maybe if we just ignored the nomad, he'd leave us alone. All I wanted was to climb into my sleeping bag, huddle close to the fire, and sleep in shifts with one of us always on watch.

Tallis walked away from the campfire, and I followed reluctantly, our eyes temporarily blinded by its brightness. We stumbled down the rock-strewn slope for about 25 feet before our vision adjusted to the dark.

It was a moonless night, but there were so many stars that our bodies cast faint shadows on the rocky ground. Stretching from horizon to horizon, the starlit sky contained as many pinpoints of light on the horizon as there were directly over our heads. Unimpeded by humidity, pollution, or city lights, the stellar canopy sparkled with a glory reserved only for those willing to leave the comfort of their urban lives and desert campfires. I was speechless.

The Tuareg had reached the top of a tall dune. He seemed to be stepping from the ridge into the twinkling ocean of night sky. He slowly disappeared on the other side into the starry pool of light. We scrambled over the last few feet of rock and began ascending the dune.

We all have a warm and familiar campfire in our lives. It is our family, friends, home, and job. It is the things we believe in: our values, our routines, our relationships and rituals. It is our habits, good or bad; our judgments, right or wrong. It is the world we know and the way we look at the world. Everyone has a campfire.

When life changes and we realize that we are in a desert, we often look for more wood to make our campfire bigger. Like Tallis and me scouring the rocky hillside for bits of ancient trees, we go to great efforts to find enough fuel to feel safe. We want certainty and routine—not ambiguity and risk. But our campfire illuminates only a small part of the real world. Sometimes we have to leave that comfort and safety, because what we need is found in the darkness of our desert night. It's as if what we seek, like starlight, can only be seen at night.

A s I struggled up the dune, I found my discomfort returning. With the Tuareg out of sight, fears began to interrupt my star-inspired rapture. A cool breeze greeted us at the top of the ridge, carrying with it the smoke of a campfire and patches of conversation. We paused for a moment and then began our descent into a small depression, where, sheltered from the wind, seven or eight men were gathered around a small fire. Most of them were Tuaregs in their white and blue flowing robes. The blue cheches wrapped around their heads and across their faces showed only their eyes. They looked up at us. One of them held a large knife.

We'd walked right into their trap. My mind began to race as I quickly tried to assess the situation. Two were dressed in shirts and jeans. Perhaps they were Algerians. Somehow, this seemed even more alarming. Were they bandits? Were they gun runners? Smugglers? Or were they malcontents, seeking vengeance on any European for years of colonial oppression?

The Tuareg who'd visited our campsite gestured to us to join the circle. Their broadly smiling faces convinced me that this was a trap with no way out. In my panic I'd failed to notice that something was cooking over the fire. It looked like a miniature antelope, and it smelled delicious. The man with the knife began slicing meat from the roasting carcass. The Tuareg spoke to one of the Algerians in what I guessed was Tamashek, the nomads' language. The young Algerian man introduced himself as Abdul. He translated the Tuareg's words into impeccable French:

"Bienvenue à notre camp. Faites-nous l'honneur d'être nos invités à ce banquet."

Tallis, who spoke only a little French, didn't need me to be his interpreter. His stomach never betrayed him. He could see that we were the guests of honor at a Tuareg feast. All he wanted to know was how soon would we eat.

As the meat was being put on a plate, another Tuareg began moving the fire to one side with his bare hand. I asked Abdul what the nomad was doing, and he told me to watch carefully. The cook began brushing away the hot sand until the bread that had been baking beneath the fire was revealed. We began eating in earnest, and the exotic taste of the savory game delighted my taste buds. Tallis swabbed drippings from the meat with the thick bread.

After dinner we began to converse. The Tuareg who had come for salt and pepper spoke no real French but was merely repeating what Abdul had taught him in advance of each visit to us. In fact, he had wanted to ask for both salt and pepper on the first visit but couldn't remember all the words. The other Tuaregs thought this was hilarious and playfully mocked his pidgin French.

PHOTO: STAN ZIPPAN

Hanging out with the Tuaregs.

Another source of humor was Abdul's 12-year-old brother, Ibrahim. Abdul teased him mercilessly. Ibrahim was at that age when parts of a boy's adolescent body seem to grow overnight to adult size. Ibrahim sported the largest ears I'd ever seen on a 12-year-old. I thought of mentioning Dumbo, the flying elephant. But my nomadic friends had never seen a television, so any humorous reference would be missed. Ibrahim was actually enjoying all the attention, and I could tell that Abdul loved his baby brother. Still thinking of Dumbo, I remarked, "Avec ces oreilles, il pourrait voler." (With those ears, he could fly.)

Abdul began laughing uproariously, and the Tuaregs begged him to translate. Howling with laughter, the nomads placed their hands at the sides of their heads and began flapping them like wings. My joke had made desert nomads laugh so hard that they were now coughing and choking. I couldn't imagine any other place I'd rather be.

We talked and laughed late into the night. After the last of the firewood was burned to make a final pot of mint tea, I nudged Tallis in the ribs to signal that it was time to leave. Ibrahim was asleep with his head, and now famous ears, in Abdul's lap. After thanking our hosts, we reluctantly climbed the dune, walking in silence and starlight to the rocky hillock and our campsite. Our little campfire had long since burned out, but it didn't matter. For the first time, I felt as if I belonged in the desert.

For the Tuareg, the Sahara is their home. They know how to live in the desert. They know how to navigate across it. And they know how to help others feel at home in the desert. It's easier to step away from our campfire of familiarity if we meet a nomad in our desert of life. But how do we know a nomad when we meet one?

Hang Out with a Nomad

There are three types of nomads. The first kind is a mentor. They make it easier for us to step away from our campfire because they know the terrain we are crossing. Every new member of Alcoholics Anonymous is encouraged to find a sponsor. This is another AA member who has more experience with following the 12-step program. The sponsor helps the new members accept their situation and guides them across the desert of their recovery.

If you want to develop a spiritual practice, befriend a monk. Do you want to forgive someone for a betrayal? Start asking around—almost everyone has been betrayed, and some have learned how to leave the campfire of victimhood. If you just want to loosen up and be more spontaneous, take an improv acting class or hang out with four-year-olds.

The second type of nomad is a generalist. Generalist nomads may not have directly experienced your particular desert, but they've crossed a few in their time. They've discovered the rules of desert travel. In their own way they know that life is not a mountain. Nomads know how to be alone and how to find support. They also know that they don't have all the answers.

You can meet this type of nomad anywhere. It could be your neighbor, your plumber, your cousin, or the elderly woman who just invited you for tea because you helped her across the street. Nomads have been humbled and deflated, becoming more human in the process. If you sense these qualities in someone and suspect that she might be a nomad, ask her what is the most humbling experience she's had and what she learned from it. Her answer should confirm your intuition.

The third type of nomad is a professional who has been trained to guide others across their deserts of change. In his book *Further Along the Road Less Traveled: The Unending Journey Toward Spiritual Growth*, M. Scott Peck writes about the practice of psychotherapy: "I used to tell my patients that they were hiring me as a guide through inner space. They were hiring me not because I had ever been through their inner space before, but simply because I knew a little something about the rules for exploring inner space."

Professional nomads, such as counselors, therapists, psychologists, life coaches, ministers, imams, and rabbis, have been trained in the rules of exploring inner space, and this is where real change occurs: inside of us. Sometimes we need to hire a guide to help us cross our desert and step away from our campfire. I prefer guides who not only know the rules but have used them to cross their own deserts. I also like a professional nomad who guides from behind—one who follows me where I go and offers guidance when I need it—rather than one who thinks he knows exactly where I am, has the map to prove it, and shows me the prescribed route to the other side. As Scott Peck says, "In the practice of psychotherapy, everyone's inner space is different."

Nomads often appear when we are considering a change or needing to step away from our campfire. Pay attention to seemingly chance encounters: a person standing next to you in line at the bank, a book that a colleague mentions to you, a speaker who is coming to town, a therapist that a friend recommends. It might be that a nomad has arrived to escort you away from your campfire.

Eventually, we become nomads ourselves. We find that there is a nomad inside of us who knows how to cross our deserts of change. If it's time to step away from your campfire, maybe you are ready to guide yourself. As your eyes adjust to the dark, the vision of your inner nomad may lead you forward.

I woke up to the penetrating heat of the sun as it climbed above the mountains to the east. Tallis was blessed with the ability to sleep through almost anything, and I envied him his effortless dreams even as the punishing solar assault commenced.

I decided to visit Abdul and the Tuaregs. I reached for my

boots and turned them upside down to evict any scorpions that had found shelter for the night in my footwear. A piece of paper fell out. It was a note from Abdul. They had left early that morning upon learning from another group of nomads that the border had reopened. He wished us luck and blessings on our journey.

I woke Tallis. We quickly packed and hiked to the piste, where we hitched a ride back to the oasis. Our ride dropped us at the dusty camel market on the edge of Tamanrasset. I spotted a cargo truck being loaded with sacks of dates. An Arab finely dressed in traditional clothing leaned on a glimmering Toyota Land Cruiser, surveying the loading operation.

The Arab confirmed that the border had reopened. His truck would soon leave for Agadez, the final oasis. His smile broadened as he explained that he would accompany his truck in the Land Cruiser. It had room for a couple of paying passengers, and it was air-conditioned. He wanted half his money now and the rest upon arrival in Agadez. We quickly made the deal. Jean-Luc's money had come in handy.

We settled under the shade of a stunted palm tree and watched the final stages of loading. Word travels quickly at an oasis. A pretty brunette in her 20s approached us. She was Belgian. Her friends had been stranded at the border when it closed, and she asked me if I would carry a letter to them. I happily agreed and put the letter in my passport so that I wouldn't forget it.

Once the sacks of dates were loaded, a large tarp was tied over the cargo. From out of nowhere Tuaregs appeared, at least a dozen, and clambered up the side of the truck. It was odd to see them perched on the truck's cargo instead of on camels. We took this as a sign that departure was imminent and watched for the Arab to appear.

All afternoon the Tuaregs sat erectly on the sacks as if we would leave in a matter of minutes. As the sun began to set and the temperature plummeted toward freezing, we opened our packs and began rummaging about for extra clothes. Suddenly the door of the Land Cruiser slammed shut. Its headlights flicked on as the noisy diesel motor kicked over. Before we could stuff everything back in our packs, it took off into open desert. Then the truck's engine fired up. There was a grinding of gears and it lurched forward 10 feet and stopped. The driver looked back in our direction, stuck his thumb in the air, and shouted "Montez!" And the truck began to move.

Tallis and I looked at each other, dumbfounded. There was no mistaking him. "Montez" meant "Climb aboard." We were going to Agadez on the top of the truck, not inside the Land Cruiser.

We ran and climbed onto the side of the vehicle. Angry and bitterly disappointed, I clung to the side of the truck wondering if we would drive all night in the freezing Saharan darkness. I wasn't prepared for this.

When we step away from our campfire, things happen that we can't predict or control. That's one of the reasons why we stay in painful situations; at least they're predictable. They're less frightening than the darkness of the desert. We stay in jobs that are boring or stressful. We endure unhappy relationships. We cling to the familiarity of old beliefs and attitudes that we're ready to outgrow. One belief that keeps us close to our campfire is that we need to be prepared for any experience away from the fire. We want to take our flashlight and hunting knife along.

My family name has an impressive coat of arms that features a fierce-looking eagle, a wolf, and a knight wielding a sword. Pretty courageous stuff, but there is also a motto in Latin: *Nunquam Non Paratus* (Never Unprepared). At times I think I've adopted that motto as a personal mantra.

Early in our marriage, my wife and I went camping. I brought a bottle of wine for a romantic evening around the campfire. My young bride nodded her approval. But when she came across the safety goggles and asked what they were for, I embarrassedly confessed that I didn't want sparks from the fire blinding me. Imagine the two of us, young lovers on a beautiful summer's evening, deep in the Canadian wilderness, huddled around the crackling fire with a glass of wine and me gazing longingly at my beloved—through quarter-inch-thick safety goggles. I was prepared for everything, even a campfire that might turn evil and begin attacking me!

Never Unprepared is a mountain-climbing slogan I live by when I'm in the high country. British Columbia is blessed with spectacularly rugged terrain that is easily accessible. Ten thousand feet seems to be my optimum elevation. It's high enough for me to see glaciers and alpine meadows and also to encounter grizzly bears. I never leave home without bear repellant. I also take topographical maps, a first aid kit, and climbing equipment.

When I tackle any project, whether it's rebuilding a deck or researching a book, I am prepared as well. Being unprepared on a mountain, whether it's a real one or a metaphorical one, is not wise. But Never Unprepared is the wrong slogan for those times when you need to step away from your campfire. If that's your motto, you'll continue to cling to what's familiar even when it no longer serves you.

Always Be Unprepared

A better slogan for leaving campfires is *Semper Non Paratus* (Always Unprepared). We are never completely prepared for the deserts of life. Were you prepared for marriage? Were you prepared for giving birth or raising a child? Were you prepared to lose your job and change careers? When we accept that we are literally and constantly unprepared, it becomes easier to step away from our campfire. Knowing that we are unprepared frees us from having to cover all contingencies before we change. We can be easier on ourselves when we don't get it right, make mistakes, or fall flat on our face.

Always Be Unprepared does not mean we become sloppy and irresponsible and knowingly put ourselves at risk. It's not a New Age slogan to excuse us from responsibility. It's a mind-set that encourages us to step away from our campfire and embrace the uncertainty of life's deserts with more ease, less fear, and a sense of adventure.

It doesn't mean you shouldn't do any preparing. If you want to leave your job and start a new career, it's a good idea to have a cash reserve, see a career counselor, and get some retraining. Always Be Unprepared is a slogan to counter the need to have every contingency covered before you step into the darkness of the new and unfamiliar. We can spend too much time and energy trying to draw a map of desert terrain we're about to explore.

Here is a short exercise that can help you step away from your campfire: First, identify your campfire—what it is that you need to let go of. Second, write down all the preparations, contingencies, and plans you'd like to have in place before you move into the dark night of a desert of change. Third, ask yourself if it's realistic to implement all those preparations. Fourth, ask yourself if making all the step 2 preparations would guarantee that nothing could go wrong. If you answered no to step 3 or 4, then the concept of unpreparedness is worth considering. You may be ready to venture forth without a map or a guarantee.

T he truck picked up speed as I hung on to the side. I worked my way forward to where there was a make-shift ladder near the cab. I couldn't see Tallis, but I assumed that he was on the other side. I climbed up the ladder and managed to get my right knee on the top edge of the truck's side, but there was no place to sit down. The Tuaregs had taken every available perch on the uneven surface of the cargo. Now I understood why they had sat in the tortur-ous sun all afternoon—no one wanted to lose his place.

A couple of nomads pointed at me. I thought they were making fun of me. I was in no mood to be ridiculed. The thought of clinging to the truck all night long in the freezing desert air was bad enough. They started yelling at me and I yelled back at them. Just then, Tallis's head popped up on the other side, and he shouted, *"Duck!"*

I turned around to see what must have been the only deciduous tree in the Sahara Desert outside of an oasis. A large horizontal limb, as thick as a man's leg, was coming at my head at 40 miles an hour. I tried to get out of the way, but I wasn't quite fast enough. It caught me on the top of my head with a hard but glancing blow. The warning and my actions had turned a potential decapitation into an embarrassing bump. Now the Tuaregs really were laughing at me.

My makeshift cheche—30 feet of turquoise blue muslin cloth wrapped around my head—was unfurling and blowing off the back of the truck. The one thing I had to keep my head warm appeared to be gone.

One of the Tuaregs near the back motioned me toward him. I started to crawl across the sacks of dates. Nomads shifted so that I could pass them. When I arrived, he showed me my cheche. Someone had caught it and rolled it up. He pointed for me to sit down in front of him facing forward. When I did that, I realized that there were at least two trees in the open desert, and he pushed me forward as I ducked in rhythm with the rest of the nomads. The truck driver seemed to have little concern for his human cargo.

When I straightened up, the nomad draped one end of the cloth over my head and motioned for me to take a piece of it in my mouth. He tied the cloth around and around my cold, bruised scalp. At first I thought he was attending to my injury, but when he was done, I knew that I now sported a properly tied Tuareg cheche. The part I'd held in my mouth could be raised and lowered to protect my face from the sandstorms.

I started to crawl back to my ladder on the side of the truck, but he put his hand on my shoulder. I now had a place to sit. There were a few words exchanged in Tamashek among the others, followed by some shifting of belongings and bodies. They had made a place for Tallis as well. We rolled on into the dark night beneath the panorama of stars. Our bodies swayed in unison like dancers performing some avant-garde ballet as the truck turned, shifted gears, or drove beneath low-hanging tree limbs.

It is impossible to avoid the blows of life. No matter how prepared we are or how carefully we plan, eventually a tree limb comes from out of nowhere and smacks us on the side of the head. Tying my cheche like a nomad would protect my face from the assault of sandstorms. But the most important lesson that first night on the truck was learning when to duck.

As we move into the unknown, anything can happen. Since it's impossible to be prepared for every problem or disappointment, we might as well learn when to duck. When something unpleasant comes our way, we may need to shift our attitude one way or the other to turn a very negative situation into a glancing blow or possibly a complete miss.

Learn When to Duck

In the desert of my career change to become a professional speaker, I stepped away from my thriving corporate fitness business. After one of my first speaking engagements, someone suggested that I hand out evaluations to my audience. While most of the feedback was positive, a single negative comment devastated me. I obsessed about what went wrong and began to lose my confidence. If there's one thing you need as a novice speaker, it's confidence. I decided that confidence was more important than feed-back. I stopped handing out evaluations for a few months. I wasn't ready for the blow, so I ducked.

Ducking is a desert technique. Knowing it's OK to duck makes it easier to walk away from our campfire. Ducking the evaluations enabled me to develop as a speaker in that first year after I stepped away from my old job. That allowed me to travel deeper into the desert of my career change.

As we try new things and bravely venture away from what's familiar, the admonitions, criticisms, and judgments we have to duck are sometimes our own. We can be very hard on ourselves. Our words of self-talk can be much worse than any written evaluation someone else would give us. But ducking is not a way of avoiding the necessary deflations of desert travel. If it's time to be humbled, to accept a loss, to let some air out of our ego so that we can get moving again, then that is what we must do.

Sometimes the ducking we do is around our campfire. The sparks are flying, but we put on our safety goggles and huddle even closer to the familiar pain. Our health is failing, but we ignore the warnings. Our relationship is loveless, but we don't try to change anything. This type of ducking is called *denial*. It keeps us close to our campfire when we really should be stepping away. The trick is to know when to duck. The essential question to ask yourself is this: Does ducking this blow allow me to go deeper into my desert, or does it stop the journey?

Stepping away from the campfire is a critical rule of desert travel. It allows us to keep moving across our deserts of change. Most important, it is good practice for developing the courage and trust we will need when we arrive at a false border.

Chapter Six

Don't Stop at False Borders

Sometimes the line in the sand is important.
Other times it's just a waste of good sand.
—Desert proverb

T he truck drove for hours through the cold desert night. It was almost midnight when we finally stopped, and everyone spread blankets and sleeping bags on the sand. The next morning, the driver yelled "Montez!" again. We climbed aboard, and the truck rolled deeper into the void of the southern Sahara.

Although it was daylight, a new darkness had arrived—a sandstorm. A steady dark wind blotted out the sun, allowing only 20 feet of visibility. All day, the truck crept slowly ahead in the dusklike conditions. Tallis and I took turns sitting under a blanket for a brief respite from the relentless, stinging assault. At night the storm abated. The next day it returned with the sunrise. There had been no sign of the Land Cruiser, and we resigned ourselves to crossing the desert on the truck with the Tuaregs.

On the third morning the weather cleared, but the truck driver was in no hurry to leave. When we finally broke camp, we drove for only 30 minutes before he stopped and jumped out of the cab. I could see a couple of small concrete buildings and some barbed wire extending into the desert in each direction for a hundred yards. Farther south I could see more barbed wire and another checkpoint. The only sound was an Algerian flag flapping in the light breeze. He climbed up the ladder on the side of the truck and asked for our passports. We were at In Guezzam, the border crossing between Algeria and Niger. I noticed that several of the Tuaregs were missing.

As the truck driver walked off toward one of the cement huts, I looked around and saw what a godforsaken place this border crossing was—just a line in the sand in the middle of nowhere. Whoever was stationed here must have done something terrible to be sentenced to such a bleak outpost.

There was an argument going on in the guardhouse. A tall Algerian soldier in his 40s with dark hair and a black moustache emerged from the hut with a passport in his hand and walked to the truck. The driver was right behind him, pleading his case in Arabic. The remaining Tuaregs seemed tense. I was perplexed. Tallis was cleaning the lens of his camera. I told him to put his photographic equipment away. I didn't want to get on the wrong side of this border guard.

The guard looked up at the passengers, glanced at the passport, and then pointed to me. He wanted me to get off the truck. As I was climbing down, I remembered what André had said as he left us in Tamanrasset—"Don't stop at the border. It's dangerous."

As I stepped down, the border guard spoke to the driver in French. He ordered the driver to get back in the truck and continue to Niger without me. My mouth suddenly felt very dry. I could only manage to utter a single word: "Pourquoi?"

"C'est pour votre sécurité," he said, without looking at me.

I was being detained for my safety? That couldn't be true! Then I saw that he was holding the letter from the Belgian woman. I knew that something terrible would happen if I were to be left behind. My heart started racing. The driver climbed back into the cab and put the truck in gear.

There isn't a natural border to separate Algeria and Niger. There's no mountain range, no river, no canyon. There's not even any tribal or ethnic demarcation. It's literally a line in the sand drawn by French bureaucrats in 1960 when Niger became independent. Tuaregs live on both sides of the border. Many of them completely ignore it, crossing regularly in the open desert away from the isolated military outposts. To the nomads the border is false. There is no reason for it to be there.

As we cross a desert of change, we sometimes find ourselves at a false border. We arrive at a psychic line of barbed wire where a seemingly omnipotent guard prevents us from continuing. Borders in life are significant turning points, moments of truth, opportunities for quantum inner growth and healing.

The border guard is a part of our psyche. It is a voice of false authority. It is a part of our ego that fears losing control should we cross the dividing line between who we are and who we could become. The inner border guard lives inside our own head and speaks with a voice of authority like that of James Earl Jones. Our false borders are guarded by an erroneous belief, a crippling fear, a mistaken assumption we hold to be true. It is difficult to argue with something that we believe has power over us, even if its power is illegitimate and its logic is false. The border guard that holds us hostage is a part of us, and yet we tremble before it.

The fear we experience at false borders makes them seem to be a matter of life and death. Figuratively, they are. When we fail to move forward and grow to our fullest potential, a part of us dies. In the desert of your career, you might realize that you chose your profession simply to please your parents. The inner border guard tells you that you cannot follow your passion and do what you love. So your passion dies if you stop at that false border.

After my marriage ended, I realized that I had been in one relationship or another without interruption for my entire adult life. When I met Debra in my late 20s, I was living with Ginger. Ginger moved out in the morning. Debra moved in that same afternoon. Somehow I managed to survive that two-hour gap on my own.

So I decided to be alone for the first time in 25 years— no dating, no girlfriend, no relationship of any kind. Deciding to do it and actually doing it were two different things. The whole idea scared me. I was afraid to be alone. I was at a border. It should have been an easy thing to do. Many people spend years, even their entire lives, without being in a relationship. To some of my married friends, my border seemed like an oasis.

Know What a False Border Looks Like

The false borders that stop us may be connected to the desert rules we haven't mastered. Perhaps we need to be alone but are terrified of it. Or we might be equally afraid of the intimacy of a committed relationship. We could be avoiding a humbling deflation because we think we literally can't survive the blow to our self-importance. I once met an entrepreneur who had not taken a single day off in 29 years. Unable to stop at an oasis, he was overworked and his company was doing poorly. But he was afraid that a vacation would send the business into deeper difficulties.

The dilemma of a false border feels different from the sense of being stuck that's described in Chapter 3. While being stuck can be frightening, it often includes a sense of frustration, boredom, or anger at our inability to move forward. But a false border always creates fear. And the fear is connected to a false belief that blocks us. Together, they can imprison us in the middle of our desert if we lack the courage or insight to challenge them.

A false border does not feel false at all. It seems to completely block our way. You think that something terrible will happen if you try to cross the border, but the truth is that something terrible will happen if you don't. Sometimes others have warned us that we will eventually have to deal with this situation. We've been avoiding or dreading this moment of truth, but it seems to have finally caught up with us.

I coached a client who was trying to rebuild her life after a difficult divorce. Sherrie was in her 40s, without children, and had a good job as the chief financial officer in a manufacturing company. She was desperate to leave the small city where she had lived all her life. She found her hometown stultifying and wanted to move to the East Coast, make new friends, explore life, and start over. As a child she had loved to paint, and she now wanted to pursue that undeveloped artistic side of her nature.

But Sherrie felt guilty about leaving her parents. Even though they were in reasonably good health and financially secure, she felt a duty as the eldest child to remain close by.

I explained to her that most parents want their children to be happy. I believed that her parents would encourage her to move, if that was what she needed to do. I also pointed out that her three younger sisters would still be in town to help when needed. Her response was always the same: "If I leave, I'll be abandoning them."

Her misplaced guilt was a classic example of a false border. She had a false belief that blocked her from living the life she desperately wanted. Sherrie could not look her border guard in the eye. She was terrified. She once admitted that the shame of leaving her parents would be worse than dying. And yet she was dying by staying.

I'd forgotten all about the letter from the Belgian woman in Tamanrasset. Without reading it, I had tucked the letter into my passport. When I saw the letter in the guard's hand, I realized that he should not have seen it. He was keeping me there for his own protection, not mine. The truck started to move, and by now Tallis sensed that something was wrong. Not understanding the situation, he yelled at me, "Get on the truck, Donahue—we're leaving!"

I saw that the guard had given all the passports back to the driver, including mine. That meant either he wanted no proof that I'd been kept behind at the border, or I was free to go.

Tallis yelled again, "Get on the damned truck, you idiot!"

I began to run after it. The guard told me to stop: "Arrêtez-vous!" I grabbed the ladder near the cab, and the truck's momentum pulled me off my feet. I held my breath and hung from the metal rung. The truck moved past the barbed wire and began crossing the several hundred yards of no-man's-land between the two checkpoints. I looked back toward the Algerian border. The guard was gone.

The thumping bass of West African pop music mixed with laughter was coming out of a mud-walled hut. The truck stopped, and a very black man in a crisp green uniform came out of the hut and climbed up the side of the truck. Tribal scars confirmed what his broad nose and tight kinky hair suggested; this soldier came from the other side of the desert. He flashed a beaming smile of brilliant white teeth and welcomed us to West Africa: "Bienvenue à Niger." I took what seemed like my first breath in an hour. Hopping down, the soldier banged twice on the side of the truck to indicate that the vehicle was cleared. The truck accelerated into the Nigerien Sahara as the Afro-beat music and laughter faded in the distance.

After a couple of miles, a group of Tuaregs flagged us down. It was the nomads who had been missing when we stopped at the border. They had simply walked around the barbed wire.

Sandstorms lashed us for two more days as the truck lumbered south. As we passed through a large village, the wind let up and I could see figures scurrying about with their hands and veils protecting their faces from the stinging sand. After a few minutes I realized that this was Agadez, the final oasis.

The truck pulled into the Gare Routière. A European woman in jeans approached us and began asking questions about the border. Her French had a Belgian accent. Suddenly it

dawned on me—the letter I had carried was for her. I told her
what had happened to me and the letter, and she started to
cry. Struggling to hold back her tears, she explained that when
the border closed, the guard had thrown her group in jail.
After two days he took her friends—a man and a woman—
away. She heard gunshots. When no one returned, she
escaped from her cell. She fled to Niger and hitched a ride to
Agadez. She hoped to return to the border in a large north-
bound convoy, confront the guard, and look for her friends. I
wished her luck and sat down, suddenly feeling very weak.

B order guards are like bullies who draw a line in the
sand and say, "I dare you to cross it." Ultimately, that
is what we must do. When I ran after the truck, I called the
Algerian soldier's bluff. He no longer had my passport.
There were too many witnesses for him to shoot me. False
borders in the Sahara and in life are dangerous places to
linger. When you start to realize that being stopped at the
false border could be more dangerous than challenging the
guard, you are ready to call his bluff.

I met a couple in their early 40s who were both going
back to school. Their desert was a midlife career change.
They were beginning medical school in Eastern Europe.
There were many obstacles to overcome: finances were a
challenge, their daughters were in high school, and they
worried that they didn't have the mental discipline to pursue this type of education. But the biggest obstacles seemed
to be those in their heads. They each had a false belief that
they thought was true. So they listened to the fear that had
the loudest volume. Bill's inner border guard told him,

"You're too old to become a doctor." Patty's guard stopped her cold with the words, "Your daughters still need you."

They discovered that there was a deeper truth concealed in their false beliefs. Instead of "I'm too old to become a doctor," Bill realized that the truth for him was, "I'm too young to give up on my dream." Sylvia, after much reflection, discovered that her truth was, "My daughters need to see me succeed in a career." So they sold their house, packed up the kids, and moved to Prague. When we challenge the false assumptions and beliefs we hold to be true, we are calling the border guard's bluff.

Call the Border Guard's Bluff

If you're stopped at a false border, the voice you're hearing in your head that is the loudest, what you believe the most strongly, is usually the false belief. That is what must be challenged. It was easy for Sherrie, my coaching client, to identify the false belief that blocked her. It was so loud, and she repeated it during every one of our coaching sessions: "If I leave [my hometown], I'm abandoning my parents." What makes these false borders seem real is that they contain a partial truth that has been distorted. Sherrie's issue really was about abandonment. But the mistake was about who was being abandoned. We tried rephrasing the warning so that it spoke a deeper truth. When we unraveled the phrase, we discovered that her truth was, "If I stay, I'm abandoning myself."

As I wrestled with my fear of becoming a part-time hermit by not being in any relationship, I listened for the loudest voice, the deepest belief that blocked me from being alone. It was, "I don't feel whole unless I'm in a relationship." I wondered if there was some twisted truth in the belief that gave it power. The truth was about wholeness, but I had it backward. I realized that I couldn't be in a healthy relationship until I felt whole. I had to do that on my own. I brushed aside the border guard and headed for my hermit's cave.

Although our own physical death is a very real border between this world and the other world, many of the beliefs we have about death are false borders. Many people think that if they accept their mortality, their lives will become full of dread and fear. But the opposite is true—we become more alive the minute we accept that this journey called life really will end.

I watched my friend Steve T. as he stopped at this border. Steve wanted to believe that he was winning the battle against his illness. The voice in my best friend's head said, "We are beating this." But the cancer was beating him. I wanted him to live more fully in the time he had left by accepting that he might not survive. I prayed that Steve would be healed, as unlikely as that seemed. I also prayed that he would have the courage to run across the false border of his fear of dying. I wanted him to be brave. If Steve could do it, then when my time came, I could do it, too.

When he asked me to call Russ, I sensed that he'd crossed his false border. Although I'd never met Russ, I knew they'd been friends since high school. But they'd had a falling-out and hadn't spoken in years. When Steve accepted that he was dying, it became crystal clear what really mattered: his friends. With weeks to live, he'd found a new compass heading to follow. In the time that remained, he could live with a peaceful heart.

Sometimes we can't clearly identify the false belief that stops us at our border. The fear clouds our reason, or we are simply too close to the experience to separate the truth from the untruth. But we can still call the border guard's bluff. At this point we need faith and courage, and sometimes a little push from a counselor or encouragement from a friend, like Tallis yelling at me to run for the truck. We need faith to know that there is a deeper truth on the other side of that false border, and we need the courage to run toward it.

A gadez is where two worlds collide. West African villagers in colorful floral-patterned shirts and dresses mingle with Tuaregs in their robes of pastel blues and white. But daily sandstorms blow through the oasis as a reminder that this is still very much the Sahara. When the Belgian woman described what had happened to her friends at In Guezzam, I realized that I'd had a very close call. Now I was anxious to reach another border—the real one, the end of the Sahara Desert.

We found an empty dump truck heading for Niamey, the capital of Niger. The ride was torturous. We had to stand with our knees bent to absorb the shock of the washboard road. Every two or three hours the driver would stop and we'd stagger out to look around. The view was always the same: another dusty West African village with scrawny kids asking for "un cadeau." But we were not in the mood to rummage through our packs for a trinket or ballpoint pen. The desert and the punishing truck ride had left us without humor.

By evening the roads became less bumpy. When the truck stopped, we saw cooking fires burning and villagers eating dinner. I heard West African drums for the first time. It was hard to tell if the desert had ended, since it was too dark to see the landscape. But something felt different.

The truck drove through the night, and we slept a little when the road was smooth. As dawn appeared, I could feel humidity in the air. I heard traffic and smelled the diesel fumes of a bustling third world city. I noticed buildings tall enough to be seen from my position lying at the bottom of the truck. We had arrived in Niamey.

The truck stopped outside the bus station, and we climbed over the side. What I saw seemed impossible to my desert-weary eyes: a wide river with dugout canoes and women washing clothes in the shallows. The driver told me it was the famous Niger, the third-longest river in Africa. Like us, the river had just left the Sahara. Rising in the highlands of Guinea, the Niger flows east into the desert, where it carves a large arc across the southern Sahara, passes through the ancient city of Timbuktu, and turns south to complete its 2,600-mile journey to the sea. We were too tired to walk to its waters.

"C'mon. Let's get a taxi to the nearest hotel," Tallis said.

"As long as it has a shower, I don't care what it costs," I responded.

The proprietor of Hôtel Chez Moustache was proud of his one and only shower, across the cement courtyard. Cold water was free. Hot water cost 50 cents. Tallis took out his camera.

"I want before and after pictures," he said.

"When was the last time we actually bathed or showered?" I asked.

"Today is February 1. We left Paris a month ago. It's been

Me in Niamey, waiting for my turn in the shower.

over four weeks since you've come anywhere near a bar of
soap, and you look like it!"

"Well, you smell like it," I said, with my first smile in days.

We flipped a coin to see who would shower first. Tallis
won. I crossed the courtyard to the small, rough-hewn counter
that doubled as a restaurant and bar. The proprietor smiled
proudly as he explained that beer was first brewed in Africa. I
opened my beer and leaned back against the whitewashed
wall. I watched the water from the shower run across the
courtyard into a drain. It was brown with desert dust.

Somewhere along the 600 bone-jarring miles between Agadez and Niamey, the Sahara Desert ends. It's impossible to know exactly which sand dune is the last one you'll see or which tree is proof that you've left the desert. There is no road sign that says, "You Are Now Leaving the Sahara Desert—Have a Nice Day." Yet by the time you reach Niamey, the Sahara is behind you.

Every traveler who has crossed the Sahara from north to south can name the moment when the truth finally sank in. Whether it is their first hot shower, the first cold beer, or the sound of West African drums, they can recall the experience or moment that signaled that they had reached the other side of the desert.

Like the Sahara, our deserts of change can end gradually, subtly. It is important to notice the real borders and to stop at them for a number of reasons. First of all, a desert crossing is an event to celebrate. It is important to acknowledge our passage. We often look to others to give us praise. By celebrating, we give ourselves the praise we deserve. When we celebrate, we nourish our spirit, cultivate joy, and give thanks. A celebration highlights our commitment to being present with every journey of our life.

Another reason to stop at the real border is to process your desert experience. When a desert ends, some people can relax deeply for the first time in months or years. Others are able to feel grief or loss that they were not able to feel in their desert.

When we consciously cross a desert, we become nomads. Not only do we know how to cross our specific desert, but we've also acquired a deeper understanding of life itself. Pause and reflect on what you've learned. Just as you may have needed a nomad's support, now others can benefit from your hard-won experience and wisdom. Take the time to integrate your experience, weave it into your life, and share it.

Finally, when a desert ends, we need to question the compass heading we've been following and determine if it's still relevant to our lives. If we do not notice that the desert has ended, we risk following a compass heading merely because it's habitual and not because the direction has meaning.

When Tallis and I realized that the desert was behind us, we decided to part company. Riding with him in a bush taxi through Upper Volta, now called Burkina Faso, I saw a herd of small West African elephants. I realized that I really was in Africa, and I wanted to see more of the wildlife and less of the beaches. He continued south toward the Gulf of Guinea, and I headed westward to visit a game park. Eventually I turned south again, not so much to be on the beach but to rejoin Tallis. After we parted, I realized how close we'd become during our journey and wanted to be with him again. Being together really mattered. This is what determines a compass heading—what really matters. But I was glad that I had followed the mirage of the game parks. Having wandered a bit, I was heading south again, but for a different reason.

Look for Your Hot Shower

In the desert of divorce, for some the hot shower is when their sense of humor returns; for others it's when they can speak to their ex without fear, anger, or blame. Unlike a mountain, with its clearly defined summit, desert borders are easy to miss and impossible to describe before you get there. But you have to keep your eyes open. Whatever kind of desert you are in, look for the actions, occurrences, or attitudes signifying that your desert has been crossed, that you've reached the genuine border. The hot shower symbolizing the end of a desert is a surprise, so we can't be looking for something in particular. We simply need to pay attention to an event or a change in ourselves or others that appears to say to us, "You've made it to the other side."

I spent a summer in the south of France after my adventure in the Sahara. Although I enjoyed the beaches, the cobalt blue water of the sea, and the hot, dry weather, what I loved most was the lemon trees. Walking down a sunny lane in Provence, you will smell a lemon tree's enticing fragrance before you see the tree itself. Lemon trees epitomize Mediterranean life, and I loved my time in Provence. Since then, it has been a dream of mine to live in a climate where I can have a lemon tree in my backyard.

When I moved to Vancouver Island to rejoin my children, I bought a house near my ex-wife. The house purchase was a significant milepost in my new life after the emotional and financial struggles of divorce. I wondered if this was my hot shower, but it didn't feel like it.

A few weeks later, my ex-wife dropped off the children to stay with me. As they bounded up the porch steps, they announced that they had a present for me from their mom. It was a two-foot-tall potted lemon tree with a single ripe, fragrant lemon hanging from it. I must have mentioned during my marriage what lemon trees meant to me. I knew that this was my hot shower. I had arrived on the other side.

The lemon tree caused me to reflect on the compass heading I'd been following and question if that direction was still important. I decided to change how I related to my ex. The lemon-tree hot shower also gave me the permission to relax in a way that I had not been able to do for several years.

Not only are hot showers relaxing, but they are also cleansing. That cleansing is important after we have crossed the desert of grieving for a loved one. If we don't notice when our hot shower has arrived, we may become identified with the grief, and it can become a permanent part of who we are. A hot shower helps us to clean away the residue of our sadness and move beyond our desert.

When Pam's husband, Darcy, died suddenly at the age of 42, she was immediately plunged into a shocking desert of loss that took over her life. Overnight she became a widow and a single parent with four children to raise. About a year after Darcy's death, Pam's masseuse, Hennie, forwarded her a joke about an elderly preacher's wife whose husband had just died. For the first time in over a year, Pam laughed. Not only was the joke about a widow, but also it was sent to her by another young widow; Hennie had lost her husband when she was 38. Sometimes a nomad who has crossed a similar desert is instrumental in helping us notice when we've reached the real border.

Initially Pam questioned whether laughing so hard was appropriate behavior. But that moment was a turning point. Pam began to envision a new life. She paused and reflected on the hard work of grieving—what she had learned and the strength she had found. Her hot shower was the laughter. Now she has begun a new life.

Specific deserts of change, such as divorce and grief, have their own hot showers that we can notice if we pay attention. The bigger deserts of life, such as long-term relationships, raising a family, careers, and even life itself, also have borders that separate life stages and signal a passing.

Although the desert of parenting never completely ends, there are real borders within it that are worth noticing. The times when your youngest child starts school, starts puberty, or finally moves out are all milestones. Each one says that something is over, and we may need to make adjustments to our direction. The compass heading we follow when raising toddlers is quite different from the direction we follow when raising teenagers.

Take a moment to reflect on the deserts of your life. Are you stopped at a false border? Have you arrived at a real border? Have you recently found a hot shower that signals a change—an end to a transition or a stage of life? Looking for a hot shower in the deserts of life is also one of the best ways to keep us aware of where we are and therefore more alive and present in our life. Finding a true border brings us peace and connects us with a compass direction that matters. When we cross a real border, a new journey begins.

Loving the Sand, Wherever It Is

We too have loved the desert to the point of feeling that it was there we had lived the best years of our lives.
—Antoine de Saint Exupéry,
"Men of the Desert," *Wind, Sand and Stars*

I found Tallis on the coast of Ghana in a remote fishing village without electricity. He was staying in a 400-year-old former slave-trading fortress that had been turned into a government-run guesthouse. It was perched on rocks above the crashing breakers of the Gulf of Guinea. I arrived just in time for dinner, as the manager of the guesthouse was serving *fou-fou,* the Ghanaian cassava root dish that looks like mashed potatoes and is eaten by scooping it with three fingers and dipping it in sauce or soup. After warmly greeting my friend, I met his new acquaintances, who were mostly young travelers—Swedes, Dutch, Germans, and Brits. We dined by lamplight as the manager recounted the sad history of the West African slave trade.

Each morning we followed a footpath through lush rain forest to Busua Pleasure Beach, several breathtaking miles of

Busua Pleasure Beach, near Dixcove, Ghana.

palm-fringed sand with nothing more than a few thatched huts and a handful of sunbathers. Fishermen in outrigger canoes hauled their catch onto shore, and local boys cooked the seafood to our order. We bought cold beer at an open-air bar and lounged on the pristine sand, turning brown beneath the equatorial sun. We chatted lazily with whomever happened to place their beach towel within range of conversation. If no one sat near us, we could go the entire morning without speaking.

Tallis stopped shaving. Then he stopped bringing a towel to the beach. He quit wearing a bathing suit, content to lie in the sand in whatever tattered underwear he happened to be wearing under his cutoff jeans. Well, it was February and this was a tropical beach. I wondered if he'd ever want to leave.

Our daily lives had absolutely no variety. We followed the

same routine without needing anything special or different to happen. One day I found myself noticing similarities between the beach and the desert.

"You know, this beach is a lot like the Sahara," I said to Tallis without looking up from my beach towel.

"Hunh?"

"Well, look at it. There's sand, there's palm trees, and it's bloody hot. Hotter than the desert!"

"Yeah, but there's lots of water," Tallis responded languidly.

"Sure there is, but it's undrinkable. We have to bring water with us from the village each morning."

Tallis sat up. It was the first movement he'd made in more than an hour. "The Busua Beach Bar has drinks we can buy. So there—it's not like the desert."

It was beginning to sound like the kind of inane argument that travelers have when they've spent too much time in the tropics. But I continued.

"Well, then, the bar is the oasis we go to when we want a drink and to get out of the sun. The beach is the desert, and the bar is the oasis."

Tallis was thinking. I knew he wanted to win this argument. I was pleased with myself that I'd gotten his attention. He looked out to sea. Then he smiled.

"I've got it. This isn't like the desert because we're not trying to get anywhere. We're just happy to be right here. We're not heading south anymore. Look south. What do you see? It's ocean from here to Antarctica. We could just stay right here forever. This is the end of the road."

Tallis smiled smugly, convinced that he'd won. But his last few words stuck with me.

"So how long are we going to stay here?" I asked.

Tallis was quiet. He was thinking. His answer surprised me.

"I don't know. Part of me could stay here forever. Another part of me could leave tomorrow."

Having crossed a desert of change, we often arrive at a time in life that offers some welcome peace and stability. We make it to our beach. But it's a mistake to view the beach—one of those periods of stability, ease, or success—as the only reason for struggling across a desert of transition. Such a belief makes us mountain climbers in nomads' clothing. The summit simply has a new name; we call it a beach.

Another mistake is to see life as a continuous series of deserts we must wander across without ever arriving. That is pretty depressing. In this view we're like Sisyphus endlessly rolling his rock up the hill.

The idea is to feel that we've arrived as we journey. We must have such intense presence that each step we take is another moment of arriving. Journey and destination coexist within us. When someone asks whether we're in a desert or at the beach, the answer should be, "Yes!" In our most confusing, frustrating, even desperate, times of change, we want to simply say, "Here I am. This is my life right now. I have arrived."

By contrast, when everything is working well, things have settled down, and life is on cruise control, we want to remember that the journey continues. On some level, things are already changing again. So we check our compass and remember our direction.

We can begin using the rules of desert travel right away.

We don't have to wait for a dramatic or sudden ending of the paved road of predictability. Even if we are not in a desert of change, we are always in a desert of life.

It's actually much easier to practice the rules of desert travel in the bigger deserts of life when change is more gradual and there is less pressure. It's a good idea to practice, because we never know when we'll suddenly find ourselves stuck in the soft, powdery sands of transition. In fact, the paved road of predictability is one great big mirage itself. Life is never as predictable as we think it is.

"**S**ee the world by freighter—travel in style." I must have come across that book ad dozens of times in the travel section of *The Toledo Blade*. Now I wished I had bought the book. The ship we were approaching didn't make me feel that I'd be traveling in style. It looked like a mistake. I suspected there was a chapter warning you to avoid certain steamship companies, like Ghana's Black Star Line.

The SS *Lake Bosumtwe* sat low in the water as the small harbor taxi chugged toward it. Lengths of raw hardwood logs protruded helter-skelter from the main cargo hold. The taxi weaved between the many ships at anchor in the crowded Ghanaian port of Sekondi-Takoradi and finally pulled up beside the African freighter. Tallis and I and two other passengers scrambled up a rope ladder to the deck, and our bags were tossed up to us.

Muscular Ghanaian longshoremen, stripped to the waist, were busy carrying bags of cocoa beans from a smaller barge onto our deck. The ship already seemed overloaded to me, and it was clear that they wanted to transfer the entire barge of cocoa into our forward cargo hold.

An officer in a crisp white uniform escorted us to our accommodations. I imagined we would share a room of at least four bunks, possibly with some of the deckhands. The officer explained that the Black Star Line was the pride of Ghana, and the SS *Lake Bosumtwe* was ideally suited for our journey up the coast of West Africa. We were on the proverbial slow boat to China, except that it was going to Amsterdam by way of Dakar, Senegal.

When he opened the door to the room, I thought he was giving us a tour of the captain's quarters. There was a double bed in an alcove with a porthole you could look out of while you were lying down. Beside the bed was a large antique mahogany desk. A couch and sitting area were on the other side of the room. The floor was made of a brightly polished honey-colored hardwood that I didn't recognize. The room was spacious and spotless.

"Does the captain mind if we are in his room?" I asked.

The officer threw back his head and laughed deeply, in that way the West Africans do so easily.

"You are mistaken, sir—this is your room," he responded with a proud smile.

"But there's only one bed."

"How many beds do you require, Mr. Donahue?"

"You mean this is my very own room?"

"It most certainly is! Dinner will be served one hour after we weigh anchor. The cook will sound a wooden chime to announce the meal."

I couldn't believe my eyes. This was traveling in style. How could an aging, overloaded African freighter have such luxurious accommodations?

Taking the harbor taxi to the SS Lake Bosumtwe.

Our meals were served in the officer's dining room. The cook was from Ghana, but he had been trained in Europe. He prepared two completely separate feasts at each mealtime— one Ghanaian, the other continental cuisine. We could have either or both.

We had free run of the ship, from the bridge to the engine room. We passed our time playing cards, sunbathing, reading, and sleeping. We slept a lot. The seas were calm. The slow, gentle rocking of the boat induced an irresistible urge to nap. One hot, still, humid afternoon we were rounding the western tip of Africa, passing from the Gulf of Guinea into the Atlantic Ocean. I wandered up to the bridge to see where we were.

"So are we in the Atlantic Ocean yet?" I asked the first officer, Joseph Ashanti.

"That is the third time you have asked me today. Are you

getting impatient to go home? Have you grown tired of Ghanaian hospitality?"

I'd gotten to know Joseph and could tell he was teasing me.

"No, not really. I guess I'm just a little bored."

"Yes, life at sea can be tedious. This is not a cruise ship. But we know how to make our journey interesting. Look ahead."

I couldn't see anything, just the tranquil tropical ocean. There was scarcely a ripple on the water. Then I saw a dot, a mere black speck on the horizon.

"That is our sister ship, returning from London. We have an African sailor's game that we play when we meet other Black Star vessels at sea."

As the other freighter came into view, I could see that she rode much higher in the water. I guessed that England had nothing of interest to sell to the Ghanaians.

As the ship came closer, I noticed the crew on her decks. Then I saw that our bridge had become full of officers and regular seamen. They were laughing and elbowing each other like schoolyard chums about to witness something special. Both ships began sounding their horns. Less than a mile separated the two boats, and they were on a collision course. I recognized the game; in North America we call it "chicken."

The bridge was a pandemonium of laughter and backslapping. With only a few hundred feet until impact, the other captain blinked first and veered his ship to our left. We passed each other close enough to yell greetings. It was impossible to tell the winners from the losers. Both crews were laughing, waving, pointing, and dancing.

After a couple of minutes our ship began turning around. I

thought something must have gone wrong. I looked at Joseph and he anticipated my question.

"Best two out of three!" he said with a huge grin.

Yes, they certainly did know how to break the monotony of a long voyage; these Africans could travel in style.

To sailors and nomads, life quite literally is a journey. Therefore, they make the best of their desert treks and ocean voyages. Life can be boring, frightening, confusing, tedious, uncertain, and delightful. We don't really know what each day or each desert will bring. But we can try to travel in style.

To travel in style doesn't mean that we use luxuries to insulate us from the bumps in the road. It simply means that we try to make the most of whatever journey we are on. It is an attitude. Traveling in style is about being at peace with the constant ebb and flow of life, and embracing what is in front of us. If we are raising a family, we embrace it. If we are between jobs, we embrace it. If we are lost, we embrace that, too.

When we travel in style, we accept that nothing is perfect, including ourselves. It makes the trip less stressful and more enjoyable. When we travel in style, we don't judge a book by its cover, a dry cleaner by his job, or an African freighter by its rusty hull. We don't judge our desert by its appearance, either. There is always more to our deserts than we see at first. When we approach life as curious travelers, both the mundane and the difficult episodes of our itinerary offer opportunities to discover more about who we are and why we are here.

November 1996. It had been 20 years since I had first met Tallis and almost as long since I'd moved from Toledo to Toronto. But I now called British Columbia home, and I only saw Tallis periodically when a speaking tour took me back to Ontario. I was planning to write a book about our desert odyssey and wanted to capture any details I could. I also wanted to capture a memory of his voice. I picked him up at his mother's home in east Toronto.

"Are you going to be warm enough?" I asked Tallis.

"I don't know. But these are the only pants that fit me. They're the ones you bought me in the summer."

"Let's stay in the car," I suggested. "I'll keep the heater on." We drove a few blocks and I stopped at a park.

"I hate this weather. It reminds me of Paris—cold and wet," Tallis complained.

I tried to find something positive about that autumn on the banks of the Seine. "Hey, remember how much fun it was when Andrews lived with us?"

"Yeah, three Steves in the same cramped apartment. We kept arguing over who would be Steve #1, #2, and #3," Tallis laughed. It was good to hear him laughing again. "I would yell, 'Hey Steve' from the kitchen, and the two of you would say, 'Which one?'" His laughter turned into a coughing spell, and I waited for it to pass.

"I guess that's when we started calling each other by our last names," I said.

There was a pause. Then Tallis asked, "Say, whatever happened to Jean-Luc and André?"

"I never told you?"

"No, what?"

"There was a letter waiting for me in Paris when we got

back. I guess you had already gone to Greece with Steve Andrews. You won't believe what happened. After they left us in Tamanrasset, they drove all the way back to northern Algeria. They were about to board a ferry in Algiers to return to France when they learned that the border with Niger had reopened. Jean-Luc turned around and headed south all by himself, determined to cross the desert."

"He must have really wanted to work in those oil fields," Tallis surmised.

"Nope. He let go of the whole idea of working in Nigeria. He was trying to catch up with us. He followed our trail as far as Niamey by inquiring at each oasis. We left Niamey the day before he arrived. Can you imagine that?"

"What I can't imagine is that he wanted to hang out with us, after all you two went through."

"Well, maybe it's because of what we went through that made him want to catch up to us. Just like when you and I split up in northern Ghana; I went to the game park and you went to the beach, but I missed traveling together."

We were both quiet for a while. The reality that we would not be doing any more traveling together was hard to ignore but difficult to talk about. I was glad that my speaking tours had brought me back to Toronto frequently in the last nine months. The desert of Tallis's cancer had taken away so many things, but at least it had given us time to be together, to say good-bye, and to prepare for our next journeys, which we would make on our own. It was hard to imagine that I would write this book without him. He was the one who had always wanted to be an author.

The tape recorder shut off, and I knew that the tape needed to be turned over.

"I'm getting tired," Tallis said.

"You want me to take you back to your mom's?"

"That's probably a good idea."

We pulled into the driveway. I helped him up the steps to the front door and gave him a hug. For 20 years we'd greeted and parted with a handshake. In the last few months a handshake seemed insufficient to express how precious each visit was and the difficulty of every good-bye.

"You know what I realized tonight?" Tallis asked.

"No, what?"

"After all that work to cross the Sahara, we only spent about 10 days on the beach. And tonight, most of what we've talked about is the desert. Neither one of us can even remember much about the beach."

"You're right," I said. "Our memories were much sharper in recalling the desert."

"Why do you think that is?" Tallis asked.

"Perhaps it's because we were so focused on the journey. When we were in the desert, we never even thought about the beach. All that mattered was heading in the right direction or stopping at an oasis. I wish that all of life could be like that."

He opened the door, stepped inside the house, and then turned around.

"That sounds like a pretty good idea for a book," he said with a gentle smile, and closed the door.

Walking down the steps, I wondered how I could feel sadness and happiness at the same time. I wanted to chase the one emotion away and hang on tightly to the other. I started the car and just sat there with the engine idling. Steve Tallis and I were closer now than we'd ever been, and he was dying.

I felt as if I were at the beach and in the desert. I was where I wanted to be and at the same time in the middle of something I wanted to run away from.

Was this what being alive really felt like? Neither one of us had chosen this journey, but we were staying with it. My heart was breaking, but not apart—it was breaking open. I decided not to run from or cling to either emotion, but rather to embrace them both. Yes, perhaps this was what it felt like to be alive. I backed the rental car out of the driveway and headed toward the airport.

Tallis on Busua Pleasure Beach, February 1977.

Tom Sawyer had Huckleberry Finn. Butch Cassidy had the Sundance Kid. At certain times in our lives we need a buddy, a sidekick, a traveling companion, to share our journey—in fact, to even make it possible. I was lucky enough to find Tallis. This book is dedicated to him and to the path our lives shared.

inner border guards, 112
inner compasses. *See* finding
    your inner compass
In Salah, 44
intuition, 85
invaders, 42–43

Jarvis, Cheryl, 87
journeys
    versus destinations, 20
    focusing on, 18, 24, 25
    paying attention to, 57

leadership, 69
learning when to duck,
    106–108
letting go
    of being stuck, 66
    of the destination, 21–24,
        25–27, 28
    through deflation, 67–68
life stages, 69, 126
loneliness, 86
loss, 125
loving the sand metaphor,
    129–131
lowering your gaze, 25–26,
    59

malaria, 44
maps, 14, 18. *See also*
    compass headings
marriage, 3–4, 87

Marriage Sabbatical, The
    (Jarvis), 87
men's behavior, 78–79
mentors, 97–99
Messner, Reinhold, 75
mind-sets, 66, 103. *See also*
    beliefs/belief systems
misplaced guilt, 114
mistakes
    in beliefs, 130
    focusing on destination
        as, 28–29
    wandering
        unconsciously, 29
misunderstanding of
    unmarked oases, 54
mortality, 68
mountain-climbing
    mentality, 66
mountain metaphor
    compared to desert
        metaphor, 3–4, 12, 14
    destination focus of, 24
M'zab, 39

naming your desert, 31
natural tendencies, 76–80
Niger river, 120
nomads. *See also* Tuareg
    nomads
    journey of life to, 135
    questioning of compass
        headings by, 122–123
    types of, 97–99

PHOTO: ELLIE MATHESON

S teve Donahue is a pro-
fessional speaker, con-
sultant, and coach. He has
addressed hundreds of corporations and tens of thousands
of individuals on the subjects
of personal and organiza-
tional change, teamwork, life
balance, diversity, innova-
tion, and discovering genius.
He has worked with such
clients as AT&T, IBM, Pills-
bury, Procter & Gamble,
Bank of America, Unilever
Best Foods, Molson Canada, and Volkswagen Canada. He
was a director of the Hoffman Institute Canada for British
Columbia from 1995 to 1997. In partnership with InCourage, he developed an interactive CD titled *Shifting Sands*, an
experiential change-management simulation for organizations in transition. He lives on Vancouver Island in British
Columbia with his two teenage children.

To subscribe to Steve Donahue's free e-newsletter or to
inquire about his speeches, seminars, or consulting ser-
vices, please visit www.stevedonahue.com or phone 800-
463-7989.

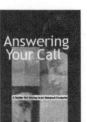

Spread the word!

Berrett-Koehler books and audios are available at quantity discounts for orders of 10 or more copies.

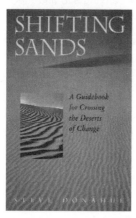

Shifting Sands

A Guidebook for Crossing the Deserts of Change

Steve Donahue

Paperback
ISBN 1-57675-280-1
Item #52801 $16.95

To find out about discounts on orders of 10 or more copies for individuals, corporations, institutions, and organizations, please call us toll-free at (800) 929-2929.

To find out about our discount programs for resellers, please contact our Special Sales department at (415) 288-0260; Fax: (415) 362-2512. Or email us at bkpub@bkpub.com.

Subscribe to our free e-newsletter!

To find out about what's happening at Berrett-Koehler and to receive announcements of our new books, special offers, free excerpts, and much more, subscribe to our free monthly e-newsletter at www.bkconnection.com.

Berrett-Koehler Publishers
PO Box 565, Williston, VT 05495-9900
Call toll-free! **800-929-2929** 7 am-9 pm EST

Or fax your order to 802-864-7627
For fastest service order online: **www.bkconnection.com**